Driving Digital Transformation through Data and AI

Driving Digital Transformation through Data and AI

A practical guide to delivering data science and machine learning products

Alexander Borek and Nadine Prill

KoganPage

Publisher's note

Every possible effort has been made to ensure that the information contained in this book is accurate at the time of going to press, and the publishers and authors cannot accept responsibility for any errors or omissions, however caused. No responsibility for loss or damage occasioned to any person acting, or refraining from action, as a result of the material in this publication can be accepted by the editor, the publisher or the authors.

2nd Floor, 45 Gee Street

London	122 W 27th St, 10th Floor	4737/23 Ansari Road
EC1V 3RS	New York, NY 10001	Daryaganj
United Kingdom	USA	New Delhi 110002
		India

www.koganpage.com

Kogan Page books are printed on paper from sustainable forests.

ISBNs

Hardback   978 1 78966 541 3
Paperback   978 1 78966 539 0
Ebook   978 1 78966 540 6

British Library Cataloguing-in-Publication Data

A CIP record for this book is available from the British Library.

Library of Congress Control Number

2020945931

Typeset by Integra Software Services, Pondicherry
Print production managed by Jellyfish
Printed and bound by CPI Group (UK) Ltd, Croydon CR0 4YY

CONTENTS

LIST OF FIGURES

LIST OF TABLES

01

Introduction

LEARNING OBJECTIVES FOR THIS CHAPTER

- Learn what this book is about.
- Learn why the next wave of digital transformation is driven by data and AI.
- Learn the basics in data science and machine learning.
- Learn how digital players apply machine learning to their advantage.
- Learn about the factors that make it difficult to succeed in data and AI.
- Learn about what it takes to scale data and AI across the organization.

What you can expect from this book

Leading digital businesses such as Netflix, Amazon and Uber use data science and machine learning at scale in all of their core business processes, but many organizations struggle to expand their projects beyond a small pilot scope. This book is a practical guide to ensure the promised value of these investments is truly realized in any organization. With direction on reinventing the strategy and vision for your business with a strong focus on data products that create measurable value, it clearly outlines best practice in ensuring return on investment for data, artificial intelligence (AI) and digital transformation initiatives. This book explains the step-by-step processes around creating an effective data product strategy, establishing data product design and delivery processes, and maturing the essential capabilities, the digital architecture and data platform in a hybrid cloud environment. Key consideration is also given to the challenges of obtaining buy-in from senior stakeholders, breaking organizational silos through cross-functional teams and using data and AI education as a powerful method for driving change. Each chapter includes key principles and tools for practitioners, common pitfalls, and case studies covering industries such as insurance, fashion, consumer goods, finance, technology and automotive. With coverage of important issues such as ensuring the establishment of a data and innovation driven culture and supporting the implementation of data products with adequate change management activities, the book enables the organizational transformation required to get ahead in the age of AI and digital disruption. This book is written for general management and C-level executives, team leaders and consultants and practitioners in digital, data and analytics departments. It will also be of value to more technical audiences, such as, for example, data scientists, architects and software developers, that are interested in the strategic part of their work, and to everyone else who is interested in how to succeed in digital transformation through data and AI. In this first chapter, we will outline some fundamental trends and concepts for driving digital transformation with data and AI which will be the basis for the rest of the book.

A new competitive playing field driven by data and AI

Data and AI create the largest wave of digital disruption so far

The world around us is changing and becoming rapidly digital. A growing number of people shop an ever-increasing variety and quantity of things online (including cars, groceries, insurance policies, watches, boats and houses). They listen to streaming music on Spotify rather than CDs and watch Netflix instead of television. They book their holidays with Airbnb and call an Uber instead of a cab. They read their books on Kindle, are in touch with their friends and the world on Facebook, Instagram and Twitter and organize their dating lives through Tinder. All of these digital platforms, services and products create an abundance of data that can be exploited to create new value.

The first two waves of digital transformation were centred around digitizing the business with software, bringing products, goods and services online and enabling social interconnections in a digital world. The more our world becomes digital and interconnected, the more data is available to feed and apply machine learning algorithms and make our machines more intelligent. This leads us to the third big wave of digital transformation, which we will refer to as the digital transformation through data and AI.

Computationally heavy methods that would not have been possible some years ago can be used today and lead to big advances in applied AI. The results are more intelligent machines that – in the specific domains they are programmed for – can sense their own state and their environment, can communicate with other machines, can learn by themselves and solve very complex problems, and act, often autonomously. Machine intelligence is expected to be a primary driver for growth in the next decades. The degree of disruption will be even higher than in the last waves of digital transformations. New sources of wealth will arise from digital transformation with data and AI. According to McKinsey Global Institute, AI will add $13 trillion to the world economy by 2030.[1]

This development is fuelled by the exponential increase in computing power, storage that is available today for a cheap price and the growing interconnectivity of people and things generating an unprecedented amount of data stored every day. In 2014, the number of mobile devices exceeded the number of people for the first time.[2] In 2019, every 60 seconds, there were 3.8 million searches on Google, 87,000 hours of video watched on Netflix, 350,000 new tweets created, 1,000,000 swipes made on Tinder, 800,000 files uploaded on Dropbox, two million minutes of calls done on Skype and one million photos shared on WhatsApp.[3] Cloud computing providers like Amazon AWS and Microsoft Azure made computational power, massive amounts of storage and scalable modern IT infrastructures available to everyone as they can be bought with a few clicks for a relatively low price via their cloud platforms. Having unlimited computing power itself does not bring much benefit unless one has data to feed the algorithms.

As a consequence, data has become a central asset in any organization and owning strategically relevant data that others do not have is a great competitive differentiator. Any digital service or product relies on high-quality data. For example, Uber needs a lot of data on how its cabs move around to tell the user when the next cab is available and Netflix requires data on its users' viewing behaviours to identify which shows are the most relevant ones for them. Another example is a manufacturing company that wants to improve its inbound logistics; it needs real-time tracking of suppliers and detailed data on which supplies are needed for production. Managing data as a strategic resource and the rise of AI have major implications for most organizations and requires new core competencies: the collection and management of relevant high-quality data, the ability to build software and apply machine learning utilizing the data in an agile way, and the constant redesign and transformation of the current business model with the new possibilities that are enabled by data and AI.

New core competence #1: Collecting, handling and utilizing high volumes of data

Firstly, capturing and handling high volumes of data in a legal and ethical way is quickly becoming a core business activity in any industry, and should be a top priority on the agenda of a digital executive and the board of management. The value of data assets plays an increasing role in the evaluation of a company in mergers and acquisitions. Not all data provides the same value, though. So far, generating data has been a side-product of doing business. Organizations now need to proactively expand and improve the collection of data assets by determining which data is of particular importance to the business and align data collection to the overall corporate strategy. This could result in the improvement of existing data collection processes to obtain data of higher quality, quantity, diversity or granularity. It could also result in the revision of processes to get approval from customers to use their personal data or to establish agreements or deals with suppliers, partners and third parties to get access to new types of data assets. Oftentimes, data cannot be acquired and needs to be generated by running experiments on websites and digital channels. Moreover, it becomes vital for all companies to integrate data and make use of this data to create value with analytics. The capability of integrating data from various sources has been already developed in many organizations in the area of data warehousing and analytics and now needs to be extended with new cloud and database technologies, architectures (eg data lakes) and agile processes and a data catalogue to make the data findable and interpretable. Finally, data is not of much value if it is not used, for example, to create new business insights with data analytics for day-to-day decision-making. A data-driven organization strives to make any decision based on trustworthy data and analysis. Many decisions can be automated with software and machine learning, which leads to the second new core competency.

CHECKLIST

Main activities in collecting, handling and using data include:

- identifying which data assets are strategically relevant for the business;
- proactively seeking permissions to use these data assets;
- improving data collection processes to increase data value;
- finding new sources of data that can be acquired;
- combining different datasets from various sources;
- processing data to make it analysable;
- applying analytics to create new business insights;
- developing a data and experimentation driven culture.

New core competence #2: Building agile data science and machine learning software products in the cloud

The second core competence across all industries is cloud-driven agile software development. All companies need to become tech companies in the future. The traditional waterfall way most companies today still create software hinders them from reacting to market trends and changing customer expectations. Many IT departments employ IT requirements managers and rely on external partners rather than their own software engineers that can directly build or change software in a fast and pragmatic way. Building, deploying and running software and machine learning models at scale in an agile way will become a matter of survival for most organizations. This includes the development of frontend and backend applications and cloud infrastructures, but also machine learning, which is often referred to as 'software 2.0'. With machine learning, software development is shifted into a new paradigm. Instead of programming software based on business rules coming as specifications from the business departments, machine learning allows computers to discover these rules on their own by identifying hidden patterns in the data. It requires new processes and roles in the form of data product managers, data scientists and data engineers, and new ways of working. Especially, the training of machine learning models can create a heavy computational workload and massive amounts of data storage that rely on flexible cloud infrastructures and cloud architecture expertise.

CHECKLIST

Main activities in building agile data science and machine learning software products in the cloud include:

- adopting agile software development and development and operations (DevOps) – 'you build it, you run it';
- introducing new roles such as product managers, data scientists and data engineers, and a strong engineering culture;
- hiring and retaining software engineering and machine learning talent;
- developing frontend and backend applications and cloud infrastructures;
- training, testing and maintaining machine learning models;
- becoming a tech company.

New core competence #3: Redesigning and adapting the existing business model

Digital technologies and AI build on each other and create new opportunities in all industries leading to unseen market shifts that generate new winners and new losers in these markets. Data, AI and digital technologies are becoming the new major source for productivity, competition and innovation, and the only question that remains is whether your company is participating on that journey. Your industry is very likely already significantly affected by digitalization, as most industries are. The third new core competence is hence the ability of organizations to constantly transform and adapt their business models to sustain their competitive advantage. Digital transformation is a change management process to renew the business model and the company culture with advanced technologies, sophisticated digital capabilities. It addresses the shifts in technology, society, customer expectations and market ecosystems. AI fuelled by the growth in the amounts of data can lead to major disruptions and shifts across all industries; for example, how and which goods and services are produced and sold to customers. Companies need to reassess their entire business and organizational model to identify how digital technologies, data and AI disrupt their business and industry. Identifying and understanding how AI transforms the industry is the basis for redesigning the business model. Business strategy needs to set a clear direction on how your company will compete and generate revenue and profit in the future and how it can transform and adapt. These changes then have to be implemented and will consequently impact the entire organization. In particular, organizational structures and decision-making processes will have to change to ensure they can take advantage of data, machine learning and software.

CHECKLIST

Main activities in redesigning the business model and organizational set-up include:

- recognizing disruptions through digital, data and AI in your industry;
- formulating and implementing a business strategy to transform, shift or adapt the existing business model;
- constantly changing software and business processes to address shifting market trends and customer expectations to sustain competitive advantage.

Digital technologies and data build the basis for the rise of intelligent machines that can make sense and meaning out of all the data and digital interactions and that start to sense, think, learn and act. A good point to start is to understand in more depth what makes a machine actually intelligent.

What makes a machine intelligent?

Computers have always been reasonably good at repetitive and clearly described tasks, and in applying strict logic and complex mathematics. An abundance of tasks today are solved by computers much faster, cheaper and more reliably than by humans. Yet, in many ways, computers in the past seemed not to be very clever. This is changing with the development of intelligent machines. Intelligent machines are able to handle situations with ambiguity, sparse information and uncertainty, thus being able to solve 'human' kinds of problems. Instead of calculating the optimal solution by using a predefined algorithm, intelligent machines evaluate different options and choose the best one.

Key features of machine intelligence

More advanced intelligent machines are able to process sensed information similar to the way that humans process information through empirical learning. They can identify objects in pictures and videos, understand voice commands with speech recognition and even decipher the smell of objects. They can go through documents and discover relationships, dependencies and hidden meanings. Instead of being programmed, they can read an organizational handbook to understand a business process and they can observe how humans conduct a business process to build their own knowledge base, and will eventually be able to handle the business process on their own. In order for machines to see, feel, hear, smell and taste like human beings, all aspects of the physical world need to be translated into 'digestible' data for machines to process, reason, and act on. Sensed information is fed, interpreted, filtered, interlinked and used to initiate further activities. This might sound very futuristic, but it is not. The rise of low-cost sensor technologies and the Internet of Things (IoT) with its connected devices enables the collection of data from the physical world without human interaction. In fact, the smartphone in your pocket has around 14 different sensors built in and transforms the signal into high-quality data that can be used by the apps you have installed.

Many intelligent machines can solve problems by understanding and clarifying objectives or even formulating their own objectives, by generating and evaluating hypotheses, and by providing answers and solutions like a human would do – unlike a search machine, which gives a list of results back to the user. Problems do not need to be provided in a specified machine-readable format, they can be simply formulated in natural language or even normal speech. Looking at the context of the problem makes it possible to interpret the question correctly. When asking an intelligent machine 'What is the best restaurant?' it should understand that I am probably looking for a nice restaurant that is not too far away from me. Increasingly, intelligent machines can even adapt their own algorithms through self-learning based on the results that they achieve and the changes in the environment they observe. Based on the outcomes of an action, they can learn and improve their problem solving. This is particularly effective in games like chess or go, in which an intelligent machine can play millions of games against itself and learn from it before it faces a human player.

Finally, intelligent machines can act, by visualizing and providing the responses to a human decision-maker or by informing or even commanding a human to execute certain activities. More and more often, intelligent machines even completely autonomously execute a business process or any other action. Based on the results of the actions, intelligent machines are able to re-calibrate their goal setting. There can be many different techniques that are needed to make a machine intelligent. The most notable one so far is machine learning.

Machine learning is at the heart of AI today

AI is the ability of a machine to perform tasks that are usually associated with human intelligence, such as learning from experience, drawing conclusions from different observations, and exercising creativity. Machine learning is currently the most important sub-discipline of AI. A machine learning application analyses the data collected using various algorithms and statistics and derives patterns from it to program itself. This enables computers to write their own software code without being explicitly instructed – by simply observing what happened in the past, which usually requires a lot of high-quality data. There are a number of types of machine learning, which will be explained in the following sections.

SUPERVISED LEARNING

Supervised learning is the most popular type of machine learning and requires a target variable that should be predicted. For instance, if you want to predict the temperature, the temperature is your target variable. The training data used for supervised learning is labelled. Famous examples for supervised learning include pictures of animals that are labelled eg 'cat', 'dog' and 'horse'. The task for the machine learning algorithm is to use these labelled pictures to be able to classify unlabelled animal pictures as 'cat' and so forth.

Predicting in machine learning does not necessarily refer to predicting what will happen in the future (like in the example of weather predictions). It can also refer to predicting something you do not know with the data that is available to you. For example, if you know the income of some of your customers, you might be able to predict the income of all your customers. Typical methods in supervised learning are regression for predicting a continuous target variable (eg temperature in Celsius) and classification for predicting categorical variables, as in the animal picture classification example.

UNSUPERVISED LEARNING

Unsupervised learning does not require any labelling of training data. Free from the constrictions of preset targets, the algorithm is likely to find unexpected patterns in the given data. Typical applications include data clustering and anomaly detection. An example of putting clustering algorithms into practice would be the refined structuring of customers into groups according to features that you have not previously been aware of and which you could use to tailor your marketing activities. Similarly, unsupervised learning can be applied to market basket analysis to determine which products are suitable for cross-selling depending on the customer's purchasing behaviour. Anomaly detection in turn can be used to detect anomalies in bank transactions to investigate fraud. Frequently used algorithms comprise principal component analysis and k-means clustering.

REINFORCEMENT LEARNING

Reinforcement learning substantially differs both from supervised and unsupervised learning. The machine is referred to as an agent and watches its environment, makes decisions and obtains a reward or a penalty depending on the outcome of its decisions. The agent's aim is to maximize the rewards or minimize the penalties over time, which it achieves through learning via trial and error. Prominent applications include major triumphs in the area of games, such as AlphaGo for Go or AlphaZero for chess, both developed by Google's DeepMind. Typical methods for reinforcement learning include Markov decision processes and Q-learning.

DEEP LEARNING

Deep learning is a subset of machine learning that uses artificial neural networks. It can comprise supervised, unsupervised or semi-supervised learning. The concept of artificial neurons is inspired by biological neurons that are strongly interconnected and transmit signals from one to another, thereby conveying information and forming the groundwork for the human brain to function. Artificial neurons also form connections and can consist of several (deep) layers, while each neuron obtains an input signal from one or more neurons and transmits an output signal to one or more other neurons. The way and direction in which these artificial neurons are interconnected characterize the different methods of deep learning, such as convolutional and recurrent neural networks. Convolutional neural networks consist of highly connected artificial neurons and are often applied to image recognition as well as natural language processing. Recurrent neural networks are powerful tools for tasks with a temporal and/or predicting component, eg in predicting time series or in sentiment analysis.

How to train, test and run a machine learning model

As discussed, most AI applications are based on supervised machine learning. Training a supervised machine learning model requires suitable pre-processed training data, a selection process to determine which features are adequate to inform the model, the application of the machine learning algorithm, and finally the testing and validation processes to determine that the machine learning algorithm really works and to refine and improve it further (see also Figure 1.1).

In a typical machine learning project, the steps are as follows. First, the data scientists receive a set of unstructured training data that they explore, visualize and pre-process in a way that ensures that the data is clear from mistakes and suitable for the problem at hand. This crucial step is more often than not the most time-consuming part of a machine learning project. Second, the feature variables that shall be used as input variables are determined manually or by another algorithm, such as the principal component analysis mentioned above. Third, we need to apply the models to the training dataset in order to

FIGURE 1.1   How to train, test and apply a machine learning model

Input: Feature variables	Step 3: Find models that best predict the target variable	Output: Target variable(s)
eg customer characteristics	**Predict**	eg customer purchases
Step 1: Prepare data	**Step 4:** Test the prediction quality of models with test data	**Step 5:** Apply model in real life
Step 2: Identify features		

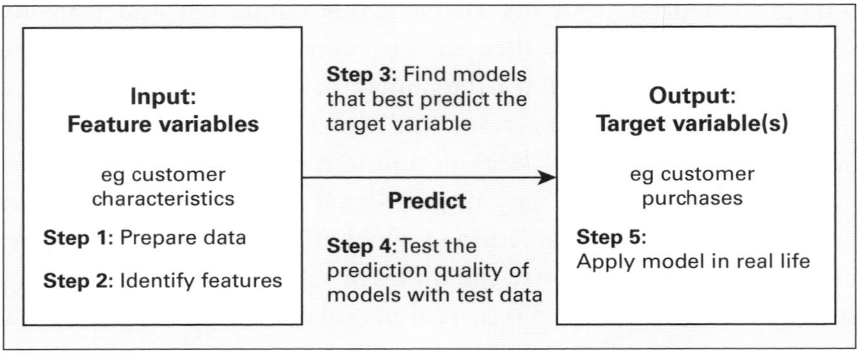

determine the best model. Fourth, we need to validate the model by using test data that the algorithm has not seen before to verify that it is generalizable and has a good prediction quality. Finally, in the fifth step, the best model is then deployed and applied in real life to new data to make predictions that are used in practice.

What comes next in AI?

There are a number of exciting new and upcoming developments in AI. The first one is the rise of corporate knowledge graphs that allow virtual assistants like Siri and Alexa to connect knowledge from different domains and, thus, be intelligent beyond a single domain. Google's Duplex is a voice assistant that calls up restaurants to reserve a table for you and is one of the current highlights of what smart assistants can do for humans.

Furthermore, quantum computing will enable machines to make computations at incredible speed; however, the actual applications are still developing. We will see more and more decision-making systems that are built on top of machine learning algorithms to combine the results of several algorithms and to decide what to do with them in the wider context. Finally, there will be a higher demand for transparency of machine learning algorithms when AI will make a higher number of decisions and mission-critical tasks will be performed by machines. How machine learning and AI are already used by leading digital companies today is the subject of the next section.

How digital players use machine learning to their advantage

Becoming a data-driven company can be a long journey, and as an organization it is a major advantage to be young. For those companies that were founded in the internet age, using data to optimize every single part of the business comes naturally. Big internet players like Google, Netflix, Amazon, Uber, Airbnb, Booking and Spotify have it in their DNA to use machine learning in every business process and every geography in which they operate. In this section we will look more closely at what they actually do.

AI first at Google

Google has been continuously transforming its products towards AI- and machine learning driven services. The Google search engine started out with algorithms based on a set of rules and is now working with deep learning. The Smart Reply service uses machine learning to suggest email replies. Google Assistant makes appointments over the phone and some people have suggested that it is the first computer that passed the Turing test.[4] The Turing test, developed by Alan Turing in 1950, is passed when humans communicate with a machine and cannot tell if it is a human or machine they are communicating with. Several research initiatives use AI, eg searching for exoplanets, predicting risk factors for heart diseases, and creating songs and drawings.[5] In line with this strategic focus on AI services, the CEO Sundar Pichai termed the current technological changes the move towards an 'AI-first world'.[6]

How Netflix applies machine learning to disrupt Hollywood and TV

Netflix not only use machine learning to generate your entire start screen with personal recommendations of movies based on the history of what other people similar to you have watched, they also personalize each artwork to depict the movie in the way you would most feel attracted to, using thousands of video frames from an existing movie.[7] They even use data analytics to know who will watch a new movie before it is even produced and predict the best location to shoot the movie, and they speed up post-production quality checks using automated algorithms that identify parts of the movie that require adjustment.

Data-driven shopping and supply chain at Amazon

Amazon have integrated AI and machine learning into the company's core business model. Flagship AI products include smart home assistant Alexa, the cashier-less grocery store Amazon Go, and the Amazon Prime Air delivery drone. These flagship products use several different machine learning methods, including neural networks making use of data derived from microphones, cameras and sensors. For their retail platform, Amazon aggregate and analyse purchasing data on products to predict demand and purchasing patterns, identify fraudulent purchases, examine browsing and purchasing data to provide customized recommendations on product and promotions, and optimize their entire inbound and outbound supply chain using near real-time analytics.[8]

Tracking the driver and user at Uber

Every day, Uber analyse millions of trips in 700 cities around the world, generating information on traffic, preferred routes, estimated times of arrival/delivery and drop-off locations, with the aim to deliver a seamless user experience to their customers.[9] Uber predict when and where there will be demand for transportation and use this information to send alert messages to their drivers, to warn them about the upcoming demand and to increase prices during peak hours to ensure that there is enough supply for the demand. The second area for machine learning at Uber is optimizing the time it takes to complete a journey by optimizing the route and by sending drivers proactively to pick-up points where there is a lot of demand predicted. Uber use natural language processing and machine learning in their chats with the drivers to make it as easy as possible for the driver to communicate with Uber, with suggested 'one click' options. Finally, Uber also use machine learning to calculate the best route and decide who to drop off first, when several customers share a ride in the Uber pool service.

Travel online with data at Airbnb and Booking.com

Airbnb and Booking.com set out to leverage official information on accommodation and individual travel experiences to generate major online marketplaces for the hospitality industry. Both companies developed a set of machine learning models to create a highly personalized travel planning and review journey.

Booking.com created recommendation algorithms to suggest travel destinations. They also developed machine learning models concerning user flexibility, context of travel and summary of reviews.[10] For example, they use machine learning to create a user preference profile that contains the likelihood of user flexibility in terms of different aspects of the journey. A user with a high flexibility would get more suggestions for alternative dates or destinations, while a user with a low flexibility would regard this as distracting and therefore does not receive these alternative suggestions.

Airbnb use machine learning models to help guests find suitable accommodation according to their preferences and to support hosts to improve their listings. Airbnb Search uses deep learning to personalize the search experience and to provide guests that search for accommodation in a particular location with a shortlist of ranked suggestions.[11]

How Spotify replaced the radio

Spotify have excelled at providing a personalized experience in listening to and finding new music. The company use a variety of methods in machine learning by analysing different kinds of information associated with a song.[12] However diverse the sources and types of information, though, the overall goal is to sort songs into categories. First, Spotify analyse the available text information affiliated with a song, eg the genre, with natural language processing. Second, they associate the respective song with other songs that users with similar taste have been listening to. Third, they analyse the raw audio data related to a song, which may contain elements that the listener is not completely aware of. These different types of information allow them to label each song with tags that serve as filters to allocate similar songs to the same group, so that users receive suggestions of songs of the same group that they prefer.

What we can learn from digital players

As seen in the different examples, global digital players are using data science and machine learning at a large scale to drive business value in all of their core business processes. New tools, new types of databases and the rise of cloud computing allowed high volumes and diverse formats of data to be combined and processed very flexibly, bringing new flexibility in working with large amounts and varieties of data. New ways of working between business and IT aimed at bringing rapid business value were introduced in the tech startup world and copied to more established businesses, bringing new agility. Machine learning and AI methods entered business life with the effect that processes can be increasingly automated.

Why many digital transformation initiatives struggle

Impressed with what Google, Netflix, Amazon, Uber, Airbnb, Booking, Spotify and many more digital companies are doing and how well they perform on the stock market, traditional companies have started to react. Top executives of such companies put hundreds of millions of investments into building capabilities in digital, data and AI in the hope of getting similar outcomes. Here starts the other side of the story, which is far less optimistic: a large number of high-profile digital transformations have failed in recent years. General Electric, Lego, Procter & Gamble, Burberry, Ford and Nike are just a few examples of traditional companies that all invested large sums into their digital transformations and have failed. Investments in big data platforms did not pay off as data science laboratories struggled to scale their machine learning prototypes beyond a small pilot scope. So far, most chief digital officers and chief data officers (referred to collectively as 'CDOs' in the rest of the book) have had trouble creating enough business impact. According to *Forbes*, appointing CDOs is increasingly seen as a sign of weakness by investors as it appears that the board does not have enough digital savviness and the company is behind the curve.[13] The digital transformation must be driven directly by the CEO and the entire company should be seen as on the way to being transformed into a tech company. CDOs can only support and advise the CEO in this transition, but cannot make up for the lack of involvement of a CEO. This section will uncover further underlying reasons why digital transformation and machine learning at scale are so difficult for traditional companies, and the lessons learned on how it can be done better.

Exponential change is difficult to anticipate and challenges longstanding beliefs

Digital and AI disruption follows an exponential curve, which means that it comes slowly without being noticed, but then suddenly and brutally turns your entire industry upside down (as in the case of Nokia and Kodak). Considering that yours is a traditional company, the digital maturity of your company is probably extremely low and it takes years to see the first results. At the same time, the revenues and profits of your company are still very high since your products are in the 'cash cow' phase of their product lifecycle. So, top executives do not really feel the pain of the digital disruption that is entering your industry. Perhaps they believe that it is coming, but that is very different to real pain. Even then, it takes years of digital catch-up until the first results are seen. There are not many executives that are willing to wait that long, as most of them will have moved into new jobs by then or retired. Why should anyone risk their bonus today for something that does not impact them immediately? This will happen only if the CEO directly drives the change.

This can be supported by looking at what happens in other industries. Every month there are examples of new digital entrants that are disrupting big players in traditional industries. With a bit of research, it is possible to show your top executives the effects that digitization and AI transformation have on your particular market and industry. The expectation from shareholders and board of directors is that the board of management will take the transformation seriously. The authors could observe that board members and top executives become willing to listen and to experiment and even make painful changes as they realize that digital and AI transformation does not stop in particular niches but will affect everyone.

A major mistake that many executives driving digital transformation make at the beginning is to assume that others understand and share the same core beliefs about the success factors and changes in their industry. But they do not. Others in their company, which includes the top management, have been running their company based on the same unchanged core beliefs for decades. These existing core beliefs have been true for a while. Examples are the standardization of processes to reduce cost, hardware product centricity to ensure product quality and attractiveness, number of sold products as a key performance indicator and the number of physical stores as a reflection of market power. It might be that software engineering becomes equally important to hardware engineering and manufacturing. It could mean that data and analytics might become a central part of product quality and customer experience. It could well be that physical stores are replacing digital touchpoints. Digital disruption suddenly turns the world upside down.

So, at the very beginning of the digital transformation, the CEOs and CDOs together need to set the scene and also explain its implications, and then ask directly for the changes to be implemented to match the implications. Complementary implementation projects that demonstrate value and roadblocks that can be discussed as tangible examples can be of help.

Legacy IT systems and back office processes are big hurdles for digitization

Companies have to live with a lot of legacy systems. For example, up to 90 per cent of the average bank's IT budget is spent on maintaining those systems. To avoid replacing the legacy systems, banks have often built new applications on top of old ones and added new interfaces. A typical retail bank has to manage and monitor between 300 and 800 back office processes. Many of these are redundant tasks, creating excessive manual processing with slow response times.

Very simply speaking, business processes can be divided into two categories, namely, front office processes, which are all customer interfacing business processes, and back office processes, which are all business processes that have no customer touchpoints. The customer does not usually see the back office.

Even if your customer does not see what is going on, digital transformation of the back office is very important to your business success. A great customer experience is often not possible without efficient and effective back office processes. For instance, when the stock level and availability for each product is captured digitally, it is ensured that the customer always has accurate information in real time. Second, making your back office running more efficient with digital transformation can save a lot of costs and make operations run smoother and leaner. A lot of additional service staff can be saved if machines can help answer a large proportion of customer service requests. And third, digital transformation makes a back office more effective, which can assist the business, for instance, to optimize the supply chain management, to prevent fraud, manage business performance better, optimize physical assets, create the highest value with available human resources and better manage finances.

In essence, executives should avoid focusing all their digital innovation efforts only on what is shiny and visible to the customers. The inner core of a business and the digital architecture is often the stronger competitive differentiator, even if that is not directly seen from the outside.

Data and AI are the main ingredients of digital transformation, but not the only ones

Digital transformation needs to change a lot of key aspects of an organization all at the same time, which makes it so incredibly difficult: business model, culture, capabilities, technologies, processes, partnerships and many other aspects. The range of digital technologies that form the bottom of the change can be very wide: from well-known frontend and backend software technologies, RFID chips and sensors, to blockchain and quantum computing. All of these technologies have one effect: they produce new volumes of data that can be fed into the machines, and they require more sophisticated orchestration. This is where artificial intelligence becomes essential. Anything digital is a result of data and algorithms plus something else on top, eg a screen where the result is shown to a user. It means that there is no digital transformation without data transformation. This is the most important formula for data, analytics and AI executives. Any chief digital officer that says 'We will deal with data and AI later since we have other more important priorities for digital transformation at the moment' misses out that anything else digital he wants to do requires data and AI. Unfortunately, in very product-driven companies this happens very often. Communicating this simple formula and explaining it with tangible examples reminds everyone that data is a key ingredient to any form of digitization effort and digital product. The fact that we always need something more than data and AI puts any data executive at a strategic disadvantage. Simply put: if others don't do their job, you will fail too. So you had better choose projects where you can rely on the other ingredients to make your data products work. The best algorithm to determine the optimal pricing of goods sold does not add much benefit, if the results of the algorithm are not used inside an e-commerce portal to improve pricing. Digital technologies create the basis for artificial intelligence and, vice versa, data and AI are central to any digital transformation.

Why so many algorithms stay in the lab

Large organizations started hundreds of machine learning and data science projects as the business world realized that machine learning, big data and AI can generate new value from large amounts of data generated through digitalization of the business. Accordingly, companies hired data scientists and expected them to deliver data products that addressed their core business problems. While many use cases and small pilots worked inside a laboratory setting, transporting them outside, to the real world, made them suddenly break and collapse. Only a tiny fraction of these pilots have been successfully scaled and deployed to production. There are a number of reasons for this:

- The field of AI and machine learning is evolving quickly and currently lacks standardization. The resulting high number of constantly changing frameworks and tools creates friction and additional efforts that make it difficult to streamline the data product lifecycle from concept to development to delivery.

- Organizational and cultural barriers prevent data products from reaching their full potential. Teams who develop data products often do not work alongside the business departments due to organizational restraints and cultural barriers. This compounds the ability of the data scientists to fine-tune the model with the business requirements at hand. Similarly, there is often friction between data scientists and data engineers, because data scientists often focus on building machine learning models while spending less time on optimizing their code writing, which makes it more difficult for data engineers to deploy machine learning models to production.

- Administrative company processes involving risk management, security, data protection, and other regulatory and compliance requirements are more often than not very cumbersome for data products and take a long time. The reason is that established processes are lacking, simply due to the new and unique requirements of data products that are also subject to constantly changing regulatory frameworks. Sometimes a successful proof of concept might not be developed further because the underlying data collection scheme would infringe requirements set out by the General Data Protection Regulation (GDPR). Finally, slow and complex purchasing and approval processes make it difficult to have a fast time-to-market.

- A technological and cultural rift often exists between teams who develop data products and teams who are responsible for IT operations. In many companies, IT operations involve different toolsets and architectures with a lot of legacy systems and no implementation of cloud technologies yet. In contrast, data scientists use newly developed open source frameworks and cloud technologies. However, both IT operations and data product teams have to work jointly together to deploy data products to production. This also involves adapting the existing deployment and operations processes that are often unfit for continuous delivery and integration that data products require.

- Data inevitably changes over time. Consumption patterns might change or errors in the dataset might accumulate. Qualitative issues with the models and data change over time. Constant monitoring and updating of the data and models is therefore necessary.

- There is a lack of skills and understanding in cloud, software and AI engineering, as it is not the core competence of most organizations. Tech talents are not attracted to a non-tech culture where they do not get the recognition and the necessary environment and executive support to thrive.

The situation is further aggravated when the typical data scientist has usually joined the company only recently, does not know how the company is running and lacks the personal network.

All these issues need to be dealt with to succeed in data and AI. That is why so many organizations struggle to put their data products into production.

How to scale data and AI across the organization

What it takes to succeed in data and AI

We have discussed the difficulties that organizations run into when driving the next wave of digital transformation through data and AI. Organizations are faced with many 'chicken-and-egg' problems at the starting point of the transformation that have to be overcome. Digital transformation through data and AI needs to be driven from four distinct perspectives, as displayed in Figure 1.2.

The strategy perspective addresses how the company's business model needs to adapt and is reinvented through data and AI. The product perspective focuses on designing and delivering scalable data products that can turn vision into reality. The capability perspective deals with the underlying capabilities, governance and technology

FIGURE 1.2 Four perspectives of driving digital transformation through data and AI

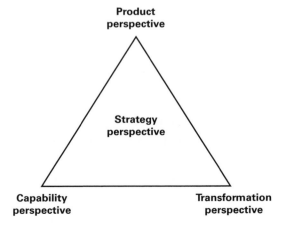

needed to make data products successful. And, finally, the transformation perspective looks at how to foster a data and innovation driven culture and at managing the change during the transformation. In a nutshell, what is needed is a balancing act of these four perspectives. All aspects need to be tackled in a coordinated effort and should fully support each other, which creates an enormous alignment challenge. The rest of this book will focus on these four perspectives.

CHECKLIST

Driving digital transformation through data and AI requires four perspectives:

- **The strategy perspective:** The overarching strategy and vision forms the core of the digital transformation as it lays out how the business should be reinvented.

- **The product perspective:** Designing and delivering products is necessary to translate vision into tangible deliverables and integrate them into the business.

- **The capability perspective:** Building capabilities in the form of skills, structures, roles, processes and governance, and implementing technologies in the form of the data platform and architecture are essential to design and deliver data products.

- **The transformation perspective:** Changing company culture and transforming the business is the ultimate goal and is needed to drive the adoption and success of scaling data science and machine learning across all core business processes.

The strategy perspective

The strategy perspective examines how profoundly data and AI will disrupt the market your company operates in. This could mean that customer expectations, products, distribution channels, supply chains and competitors are changing. Your business model and strategic positioning in the marketplace must be adapted to these new realities. Consequently, core beliefs on which your company has been based for decades are suddenly reworked, which can be a very cumbersome and often painful process for any organization. A new strategy and vision define the path for a successful digital transformation through data and AI and sets the priorities for all other perspectives (product, capability, transformation). At its heart, the strategy perspective encompasses the realization and acceptance of truly transformative change in order to survive as a company and sets in motion the necessary actions.

We will cover the strategy perspective in this chapter:

Chapter 2: Strategy and vision for data and AI

The product perspective

The most tangible part of digital transformation through data and AI is the product perspective. Data products are software applications with a strong focus on data science and machine learning. The goal of data products is to provide an overall solution to a business problem and therefore there are many feedback loops and interactions with customers and users when designing and building the product. Counter-intuitively, data products can contain other frontend and backend software functionalities in addition to the machine learning and data science functionalities as they aim to solve a business problem holistically. Implementing a data product might even require changes in business processes. Every data product should have some accompanying product marketing by the product manager and a product roadmap with a feature backlog. Every data product has a product lifecycle, which follows several phases from design, prototyping, development and deployment, operation and maintenance to end of life. After deployment, the data product might be potentially scaled to other business areas.

We will cover the product design and delivery perspective in these two chapters:

Chapter 3: Data product design

Chapter 4: Data product delivery

The capability perspective

The third perspective on digital transformation through data and AI is capability. The data capability strategy outlines which capabilities need to be grown in order to be able to deliver the data product portfolio. There are a number of essential capabilities that need to exist or be created in order to be able to design and deliver data products successfully. The data and AI organization deals with the organizational set-up, and the roles and processes necessary to ensure that these core capabilities are developed. The data platform makes critical technologies and architecture components available to the rest of the organization. It ensures a common state-of-the-art data analytics and AI toolbox that can be used for developing, deploying and operating data products. This means that an idea for a data product can be explored and then later operated on the same technological environment. The data platform provides a central data storage for productive data as part of a joint data lake and data catalogue and standardized accesses and interfaces to legacy IT systems. On top, data and AI governance processes can be defined to ensure that data and AI can be trusted.

We will cover the capabilities and technology perspective in these two chapters:

Chapter 5: Capabilities and agile organization

Chapter 6: Technology and governance

The transformation perspective

The final perspective on driving digital transformation through data and AI is transformation to drive adoption of data science and machine learning at scale. If organizations want to keep pace, they will need to radically question and adapt their business model, vision, values and structures. Data and AI bring new ways of working and often disrupt existing business processes. This can even lead to shifts of power between internal and external stakeholders. Especially in large traditional companies, there is likely to be enormous resistance to the change, as many employees and managers that were running the business in the past may not feel comfortable with, and might even feel sidelined by, the new strategy and vision. Throughout the transformation, the progress needs to be tracked and impediments managed and given a lot of top executive attention. The strategy and vision need to be translated into objectives and key results that are measured. The CEO and top executives must drive the business vision and transformation strategy, keeping communication transparent and tailored to each group, and involving senior and middle management and employees. Efforts by individuals on any level should be encouraged and recognized. Training and education can play an important role in gaining support and developing digital talent internally, while recruiting and retaining digital talent at all levels should be at the top of the list for top executives. A culture of learning, experimentation and innovation, and data and AI driven decision-making needs to be spread across the organization. Data and AI governance, quality and control mechanisms can enable trust to be built and support it. We need to address the cultural challenges that are posed by data and AI with adequate transformation and change management, and the right types of change management activities that complement the build of data products and the growth of capabilities.

We will cover the transformation perspective in this chapter:

Chapter 7: Transformation and culture

Summary and conclusion

As we have seen in this chapter, data and AI are integral parts of any digital transformation. Technologies in AI are ready to be used. Many digital players are already advanced in realizing value from data and AI, and more traditional players are struggling to make major changes to how their company operates and to deal with challenges such as legacy IT systems and unfit processes. Each of the four complementing perspectives, ie the strategy, product, capability and change perspectives, need to be addressed in a joint orchestrated strategy to succeed in digital transformation through data and AI. How to achieve this will be covered in the next chapter, which focuses on the strategy perspective.

Notes

1 Bughin, J, *et al*, Notes from the AI frontier: Modeling the impact of AI on the world economy, McKinsey Global Institute, Discussion Paper, 2018. www.mckinsey.com/featured-insights/artificial-intelligence/notes-from-the-ai-frontier-modeling-the-impact-of-ai-on-the-world-economy (archived at https://perma.cc/VZD9-HJ5U)

2 Cowhey, P F and Aronson, J D, *Digital DNA: Disruption and the challenges for global governance*, 2017, Oxford University Press

3 Lewis, T, Internet statistics 2019: E-comm, coverage, usage, speed and more [Blog], 5 April 2019. https://hostsorter.com/internet-statistics/ (archived at https://perma.cc/V6FK-LBTD)

4 Neufeld, E and Finnestad, S, In defense of the Turing test, *AI and Society*, 2020, pp 1–9; O'Leary, D E, Google's Duplex: Pretending to be human, *Intelligent Systems in Accounting, Finance and Management*, 2019, 26(1), pp 46–53

5 Google AI, Advancing the state of the art, 2019. https://ai.google/research/ (archived at https://perma.cc/5Z9W-SA92)

6 Pichai, S, Making AI work for everyone [Blog] 17 May 2017. https://blog.google/topics/machine learning/making-ai-work-for-everyone/ (archived at https://perma.cc/QRQ5-Y377)

7 Yu, A, How Netflix uses AI, data science, and machine learning – from a product perspective, [Blog], 27 February 2019. https://becominghuman.ai/how-netflix-uses-ai-and-machine learning-a087614630fe (archived at https://perma.cc/7E4C-A63R)

8 Camhi, J and Pandolph, S, Machine learning driving innovation at Amazon, *Business Insider Deutschland*, 17 April 2017. https://www.businessinsider.com/machine-learning-driving-innovation-at-amazon-2017-4?r=US&IR=T (archived at https://perma.cc/9QNS-VEG7)

9 MSV, J, Managing machine learning models the Uber way, *Forbes*, 26 June 2019. www.forbes.com/sites/janakirammsv/2019/06/26/managing- machine-learning-models-the-uber-way/#61a6aeec4ae4 (archived at https://perma.cc/P7QK-MBJG)

10 Bernardi, L, Mavridis, T and Estevez, P, 150 successful machine learning models: 6 lessons learned at Booking.com, in *Proceedings of the 25th ACM SIGKDD International Conference on Knowledge Discovery and Data Mining*, July 2019, pp 1743–51

11 Haldar, M, *et al*, Applying deep learning to Airbnb search, in *Proceedings of the 25th ACM SIGKDD International Conference on Knowledge Discovery and Data Mining*, July 2019, pp 1927–35

12 Ciocca, S, How does Spotify know you so well? [Blog] 10 October 2017. https://medium.com/s/story/spotifys-discover-weekly-how-machine learning-finds-your-new-music-19a41ab76efe (archived at https://perma.cc/D2A8-BSUS)

13 Woods, D, When does a chief digital officer signal weakness? *Forbes*, 28 September 2014. www.forbes.com/sites/danwoods/2014/09/28/when-does-a-chief-digital-officer-signal-weakness/#47d007cb5764 (archived at https://perma.cc/3EB3-WQWW)

02

Strategy and vision for data and AI

LEARNING OBJECTIVES FOR THIS CHAPTER

- Learn why a new strategy and vision are essential.
- Learn how to rethink the current corporate strategy and business vision.
- Learn how to create a data product strategy.
- Learn how to define a capability strategy.
- Learn how to build a transformation strategy.
- Learn how to combine all four into a joint transformation roadmap.
- Learn how to secure enough funding for your initiative.
- Learn how to close the gap between strategy and reality.

Key principles for creating the strategy and vision

The previous chapter outlined the fundamental changes driven through data and AI. Digital transformation through data and AI has already started to shift the current industrial landscape. Data and AI make up an innovative, complex and cross-functional discipline. It is an absolute necessity to align managers and employees across the business to foster a joint and orchestrated effort to implement the data and AI transformation effectively. A joint strategy and vision for data and AI that is shared across the organization is the basis for change. It is a massive task to create a new strategy and vision for driving digital transformation through data and AI and requires a strong willingness among the company's leadership to truly reinvent the company.

The new strategy and vision determine how an organization plans to benefit from data and AI, positions itself in the new competitive landscape and how it wants to get there. As the strategy and vision forms the core of the transformation, it lays out how the business model is supposed to evolve, which data products and capabilities will be of strategic importance and how the transformation change will be managed. The strategy and vision should be executable with sufficient resources planned and a feasible roadmap. Without it, there is a risk of missing out on the new business opportunities created by data and AI in your industry, slowing down the digital transformation progress, allocating resources ineffectively, quickly losing the board's attention and making change management far more difficult to achieve.

Based on the authors' collective experience, an effective strategy and vision can be designed in four phases addressing the different perspectives of data and AI: reinventing the corporate strategy and business vision; creating the data product strategy; deriving the capability strategy; and developing the transformation strategy.

A strategy and vision for driving digital transformation through data and AI revises the current strategy and vision of the company and readjusts it to the new realities in the industry. It addresses the four distinct perspectives of strategy, product, capabilities and transformation.

FIGURE 2.1 The four phases of developing a strategy and vision for data and AI

Strategy and vision can be approached in four phases:

1 **Reinventing the corporate strategy and business vision:** How is your industry affected through data and AI? Do your current business model and corporate strategy need to be adapted? What should the business vision and corporate strategy be for the age of AI?

2 **Creating the data product strategy:** In which business areas and for which purposes should data products be designed and developed to best support the vision and strategy?

3 **Deriving the capability strategy:** Which capabilities and technologies are needed to deliver the vision and strategy? Which competences have to be built and how should the organization be designed?

4 **Developing the transformation strategy:** What are the change management activities needed to implement the strategy and vision? How can the transformation of the company be managed?

The strategy and vision provide the company's orientation for how it plans to reinvent itself and invest resources in the short, medium and long term. This is not a one-time exercise, but an evolving plan for the future and it needs periodical inspection and revision to incorporate learning from the transformation process.

Key principles for reinventing the corporate strategy and business vision

The first phase is concerned with the fundamental changes that are brought by data and AI to the corporate strategy and business vision for your company. A good starting point is to investigate how your industry will be transformed through data and AI and to identify threats and opportunities. Companies should develop their own business vision that explains how they plan to reinvent their own business model, addressing the perceived or expected forces in the industry that create new threats and opportunities.

KEY PRINCIPLES

Reinventing the corporate strategy and business vision

- In most cases, data and AI create industry shifts that have implications for the entire business model and strategic positioning.
- Therefore, a new corporate strategy and business vision needs to be defined with new company objectives and key results (OKRs).
- The goal is to reshape the current business model and embed the plan into a wider corporate strategy, business vision and transformation story.

Key principles for creating the data product strategy

Second, it should include a data product strategy that shows in which areas and how data and AI create value for the business. Data products are necessary to implement the business vision and transformation strategy. A key input is the strategic priorities of the reinvented corporate strategy and business vision.

KEY PRINCIPLES

Creating the data product strategy

- A product approach for machine learning and data science should be followed.
- Data product domains should be defined as a framework to design and deliver data products that aim to contribute to the company OKRs.
- OKRs are formulated for the data product strategy based on company OKRs.
- Data products need to be managed throughout their lifecycle and can be often monetized to bring additional sources of revenue.

Key principles for deriving the capability strategy

Third, the capability strategy identifies the enablers required to deliver the data product strategy that needs to be developed. For example, a flexible cloud-driven data architecture and well-governed data and AI are usually needed to support the implementation of data products. Knowing which capabilities are needed is not sufficient. It is equally vital to examine which of these already exist (and to what degree), which ones the company is short of and how the gaps can best be filled.

KEY PRINCIPLES

Setting the priorities for technologies and capabilities

- Organizational and technical capabilities should be identified that are needed to ensure that the data product portfolio can be implemented.
- Current capabilities and technologies have to be assessed to find gaps in the target picture.
- Milestones, OKRs and resources for implementing the target picture should be developed and planned.

Key principles for developing the transformation strategy

Finally, in the fourth phase, a joint transformation strategy is developed that integrates all parts of the strategy and vision. It shows the required actions to change culture and people in a way that the data product strategy and capability strategy can work out. Eventually, the product, capability and culture change plans need to be integrated into an overarching transformation roadmap with harmonized milestones and OKRs and a joint resource plan.

KEY PRINCIPLES

Developing the transformation strategy

- A transformation story has to be developed to communicate the new business vision and corporate strategy to the employees and leadership.
- Change management activities to deliver the data product portfolio and implement core capability areas need to be identified.
- The milestones and OKRs for product, capability and culture change activities are combined in a joint transformation roadmap and harmonized.
- The implementation progress of the data and AI strategy should be monitored and tracked.

All four phases will be covered in more depth in the upcoming sections.

Reinventing the corporate strategy and business vision

When we think of AI, we usually imagine machines with many human-like behaviours and traits from science fiction movies. However, AI does not need to be human-like to deliver value. The current state of AI is certainly powerful enough to automate, optimize and redesign a major part of critical decision-making and to enable new disruptive business models. It is time to start reinventing the strategy and vision of your company to make sure that it will be well positioned in this new competitive landscape. A good start is to identify the threats and opportunities created by data and AI in your industry and use this as an input to redesign the business model and corporate strategy and to create a new business vision and transformation story.

CHECKLIST

Reinventing corporate strategy and business vision should involve:

- identifying industry shifts created by digital transformation through data and AI;
- analysing the implications of data and AI for the existing business model;
- developing a new strategy and vision for the business;
- formulating objectives and key results based on the new strategy and vision;
- defining metrics, baselines and targets for the objectives and key results.

Identifying industry shifts created by digital transformation through data and AI

Before crafting a new strategy and vision, it makes sense to spend sufficient time in getting a good grasp of what is feasible with data and AI today and in the near future and the impact on the business. In many industries, customer centricity and loyalty (Amazon goes even further and calls it customer obsession) will become paramount to remaining competitive. Moreover, products and services will become increasingly connected and complemented by software and algorithms on the device and in the cloud. The shifts that are happening heavily depend on the industry. The incremental value through data and AI will differ and come at different speeds, giving your company time to transform or putting it under enormous time pressure (see also box 'Shifts through data and AI'). Changes in the travel industry, for example, will arrive very fast, with new opportunities such as easier integration of different parts of a journey as more and more application programming interfaces (APIs) are provided by hotels, flight companies and local tour providers, but also there will be new threats, such as increased competition by new digital players with a focus and dedication on particular parts of travel (eg flights on Skyscanner, hotel bookings on Booking.com, private apartments on Airbnb, excursions on Tripadvisor, etc).

SHIFTS THROUGH DATA AND AI AS PREDICTED BY MCKINSEY & COMPANY[1]

Top five industries most affected by advanced analytics and AI:

- travel: 128 per cent incremental value;
- transport and logistics: 89 per cent incremental value;
- retail: 87 per cent incremental value;
- automotive and assembly: 85 per cent incremental value;
- high tech: 85 per cent incremental value.

Top five functions most affected:

- marketing and sales: $3.3–6 trillion;
- supply chain management and manufacturing: $3.6–5.6 trillion;
- risk: up to $0.5–0.9 trillion;
- service operations: up to $0.6 trillion;
- product development: up to $0.3 trillion.

We recommend the original discussion paper by Chui *et al* (2018) as further reading if you are interested how much your industry or function is affected.[2]

Analysing the implications of data and AI for the existing business model

An analysis of your industry should look at supply and demand in the future, how customer value, products and services might change, and the threats and opportunities for your company that arrive through these shifts. A good approach is to analyse the current revenue streams, cost structures, customer expectations, suppliers and competitors, and investigate how they might change in the upcoming years. Digital transformation through data and AI should not focus solely on internal process digitalization and optimization, but it should incorporate expansions of the business model and upcoming business opportunities on the customer side as well. The new business model might need to cannibalize your legacy business to avoid competitors stealing market share.

RETHINKING YOUR CURRENT BUSINESS MODEL

The current business model and corporate strategy might not be sustainable when data and AI and digital transformation change your industry. Here are five questions that can help:

- **How will revenue streams change in the future?**
  Eg from paid newspaper subscriptions to advertisement generated incomes in online journalism.
- **How will cost structures change in the future?**
  Eg from people-based to machine intelligence-based back office processes in banking.
- **How will customer expectations change in the future?**
  Eg from buying cars at dealers to online subscription-based leasing of cars.
- **How will supply networks change in the future?**
  Eg from traditional supply chains to industry 4.0 driven by IoT.
- **How will competitors change in the future?**
  Eg from traditional healthcare companies to tech companies that enter the healthcare industry (Alphabet filed 186 health-related patents between 2013 and 2017).

Data and AI create new possibilities to digitally transform the business model and, therefore, require substantial changes to be made to the existing business model. For instance, the ability to interact with customers via voice assistants might change the strategy of a consumer goods company by moving the focus of a physical product to an AI enabled product embedding speech recognition.

Developing a new strategy and vision for the business

It is important for top management to shape the new strategy and vision and the changed core beliefs together, which most likely turn the current core beliefs of the company upside down due to the forces of digital disruption. In a nutshell, it provides the answers to the two most important strategic questions: 'Where do we want to play?' and 'How do we want to win?' Executive training sessions, growth hacking workshops, interviews and discussions with executive management, board members and senior stakeholders can make it possible to clarify and formulate the new strategy and vision and core beliefs and the resulting priorities for the transformation. Some of them might be more implicit and hidden and need to be discovered through a process of trial and error. It is important to make the strategy and vision and the underlying core beliefs as explicit as possible and arrive at an agreement that is supported by the leadership team of the company and shared with the rest of the organization. The new strategy and vision will have major implications for strategic objectives, metrics, organizational structures and incentive plans. A corporate strategy builds on top of the business vision, which serves as the target picture, and outlines long-term goals for the entire organization that show the direction to evolve to achieve the new business model.

CASE STUDY
Data and AI strategy at a consumer product company

Vision and strategy

Business vision

Our vision is to become a digital customer ecosystem for our customers to enjoy digital services that supplement our consumer products and enable us to form direct relationships with our customers.

Core belief: We have to own our customer relationships in a digital world

The consumer product world is shifting from traditional retailers to online retailers. In the past, all customer relationships were managed through our retailers. In the future, consumer product companies need to own their customer relationships themselves by creating a digital ecosystem around the consumer products they offer. Data and AI will allow meaningful customer relationships to be created with millions of customers and will increase customer engagement, loyalty and conversions.

Core belief: Customer support needs to be significantly optimized and automated through data and AI to serve a broad customer base

In order to form meaningful relationships with a broad customer base, our customer service needs to be completely rebuilt with an AI first approach. Most of the support cases of our customers should be handled automatically through algorithms and business rules. Our customer service will be empowered through digital tools that make them more productive in serving our customers.

When creating a new corporate strategy, it makes sense to assess the current state of the organization with regard to the target picture to identify the gaps towards the business vision. That will help later to define new strategic objectives or refine the current ones and provide a baseline for measurements to identify in which areas the organization has made progress. The status quo assessment could include information on which skills related to data and AI are currently available in the workforce, the number of currently available data products in the organization, their current number of users, information on profit versus costs generated by them, etc. However, this sounds easier than it is as the devil lies in the details. The corporate strategy is often not documented well, it can be fragmented across business units or simply out of date and is often too broad and not operational enough. A data and AI strategy should transparently state how it changes the existing goals in the corporate strategy in a way that is easy to understand for all employees of the company.

Formulating objectives and key results based on the new strategy and vision

Digital champions frequently use company OKRs to define their goals and measure performance to align the entire organization behind shared goals. This can be used by your organization to align everyone behind common digital transformation goals and to make every business department accountable to participate in the digital transformation. The objective states the goal for the defined period, eg 'All employees should have a basic understanding of data and AI.' There are usually between three and five objectives, and for each objective there are normally between three and five key results. The key results display the details on how the objective should be achieved and they are usually quantitative and easy to measure. In our example, the corresponding key results could be:

1 80 per cent of all employees successfully finished the basic course on data and AI.

2 50 per cent of all employees installed the new internal self-service analytics tool.

3 20 per cent of all employees took part in the internal data and AI challenge by contributing an idea on how to improve the usage of data and AI in the company.

OKRs have the advantages that they are highly structured and transparent and easily monitored. They only define what should be achieved and not how it should be achieved and therefore provide the team involved with a lot of autonomy. They can be set for the whole organization and for individual teams, and for internal and external goals as well as strategic and more process-oriented goals.

Changes in the business model and the core beliefs of the company are often substantial and require a revision of the existing strategic objectives. For a travel company, for instance, a refocus on mobile technologies and personalized experiences will probably be crucial to survive and, hence, strategic objectives will need to change accordingly. If the current business model will still work in a transformed world, only smaller adaptations in the objectives of the corporate strategy might be necessary. If not, which is more likely, new objectives must be developed which replace or extend the current ones. Objectives in the corporate strategy should be specific, measurable, achievable, realistic and time bound (SMART).

CASE STUDY
Data and AI strategy at a consumer product company

Company objectives

Objective 1: Build a digital platform ecosystem to drive sales and marketing and boost customer loyalty.

Objective 2: Empower customer support through automation and knowledge integration.

OKRs resemble agile methodologies in the sense that they are also structured around a cycle of planning, review and retrospective meetings to continuously monitor and improve them. Adopting OKRs accordingly has the additional advantage of implementing continuous improvement cycles in the organization, which comes in handy when aiming to adapt the company processes towards an agile culture. Investment and steering logic of the company should be adapted to fully support OKRs and follow the principle of zero-based budgeting to best support the OKRs of any given period.

Changes in the corporate strategy and business vision will need to be complemented with the right data products, capabilities and technologies, and transformation and culture priorities. Every one of these aspects will add further objectives and key results to the corporate strategy later on.

Defining metrics, baselines and targets for the objectives and key results

Key results are measurable steps towards the achievement of each objective. Every key result therefore needs a metric that quantifies it. Adding a baseline and target for each metric makes it measurable. For instance, the goal to reach high customer satisfaction in customer service can be measured by computing the percentage of customers that deemed the service satisfactory in a survey. Another example would be the goal to improve production efficiency, which could be measured by the metric of production cost per item produced. These metrics are the basis for tracking the success of the data and AI strategy and can help you to decide on which data products to prioritize later on.

CASE STUDY
Data and AI strategy at a consumer product company

Objective 1: Build a digital platform ecosystem to drive sales and marketing and boost customer loyalty

Key results (including baseline and target):

- Increase customer loyalty measured by net promoter score from 7.2 to 8.5 by the end of the quarter.

- Reduce churn rate from 35 per cent to 25 per cent by the end of the quarter.
- Increase cross- and up-sell rate from 12 per cent to 16 per cent.
- Increase margins through dynamic pricing from 3.5 per cent to 3.7 per cent.

Objective 2: Empower customer support through automation and knowledge integration

Key results (including baseline and target):

- Increase the support provided on the website without intervention by call-centre agents from 20 per cent to 30 per cent.
- Automatically formulate 65 per cent of email and text message responses (currently 37 per cent).
- Speed up onboarding time for new customer care employees from 12 minutes to 5 minutes.
- Automatically provide answers to 80 per cent of frequently asked questions (currently 50 per cent).

Creating the data product strategy

The data product strategy is the most impactful part of the data and AI strategy. Data products can directly help achieve company OKRs of the new vision and strategy such as, for example, achieving a greater customer experience, boosting online sales volumes, driving profitability and changing the cost-to-sales ratio. A data product that provides personalized cross-sales recommendations to customers online can, for example, boost the sales volume of a company. They can turn vision into reality by providing data and AI driven software products to enable the new business model and corporate strategy. The data product strategy determines what we plan to do with data and AI in the organization to create value. In essence, a data product strategy sets the focus of where data products will contribute to your company's success. Without a data product strategy, one can quickly lose attention, spreading resources across projects without creating value and synergies.

At this stage, the actual data products are still to be identified and evaluated. The data product strategy is therefore only a high-level view of focus areas (subsequently called data product domains) for data products that should be built by determining the priorities for the data product portfolio. It will be brought to life through the actual data product design phases in each data product domain, which is described further in Chapter 3. After data product design in each data product domain, the data product strategy might need to be updated to reflect the real business opportunities. Data product ideas with a high impact but which do not match the data product strategy might be deprioritized or even removed completely from the list as they do not match the set focus and priorities. The data product strategy is usually the nucleus and foundation of the capability and transformation strategies, since it provides a pathway for how business value is generated and towards adopting the new business model and realizing the reinvented business vision.

A data product strategy for data and AI involves:

- understanding the advantages of the product approach for machine learning;
- defining the business scope and data product domains;
- formulating objectives and key results for the data product strategy;
- managing data products throughout their lifecycle;
- monetizing data products.

Understanding the advantages of the product approach
for machine learning

Looking at data science and machine learning from a product perspective rather than from a project perspective can be of help to overcome many of the previously described challenges in bringing machine learning into production and usage. Projects are typically designed to show quickly how value can be created out of data. There is, however, usually no stringent logic to continue the implementation and scaling once they have shown the value, as the product is not planned along its lifecycle. Furthermore, many data science and machine learning projects focus on algorithms and models, neglecting important aspects that are needed to be able to deploy and operate them.

Advantages of a 'product'- compared to a 'project'- based approach:

- data products provide more than a 'naked' algorithm – a holistic solution to a business problem in the form of software that runs on scalable architecture;
- a product manager is end-to-end responsible for success, from idea to operation of the data product;
- every design of a new data product needs to consider the path to go live and operation of the product early on;
- data products can be modularized more easily than can projects;
- it is easier to focus on a minimum viable product (MVP) as first output;
- data products are easier to market than projects;
- a product view is more compatible with agile methodologies;
- there is a higher focus on scaling and reusability of the product in other areas.

Defining the business scope and data product domains

The main function of the data product strategy is to define data product domains. These should be in line with the vision and strategy and contribute to achieving the company OKRs, but do not necessarily need to overlap. Data product domains can be tied to particular business functions (eg sales and marketing) or to particular company OKRs that are cross-functional by nature (eg managing quality). A major design decision is to set an organizational scope for the data product strategy in the data and AI strategy. It will depend on the mandate given, what is feasible and a number of purely tactical considerations.

For example, setting the focus on one specific business unit can make sense when:

- your mandate is limited to this business unit;
- with the resources or executive attention available, it would be extremely difficult to focus on more than one business unit a time;

- you want to show a quick success as a beacon to the rest of the organization;
- this business unit is the most cooperative and engaged;
- this business unit is of highest interest to your board or sponsor.

The organizational scope might differ between the data product strategy, the capability strategy and the transformation strategy. For example, CDOs that put a focus on their own delivery organization for data products might set a very narrow focus for the product portfolio to ensure that it is executable and feasible and acts as a beacon, while supporting the other parts of the organization in building their data and AI capabilities and changing the business. Another strategy could be the other way around. CDOs that manage the portfolio of all data product deliveries across teams residing in different business units might want to select a wider scope for the portfolio and might narrow down the capability and transformation strategy to a few prioritized business units. All combinations are possible and should reflect the mandate and the set-up of the CDO's organization. It is recommended that the business units that should be in scope for the reinvention of the business to realize the adapted business model and vision should be looked at one after the other rather than looking at all of them at the same time; looking at them all together can result in the much-needed focus being rapidly lost. There might be commonalities between business units to create synergies. Each data product domain focuses on one part of the strategy and vision. There is a case study example below for data product domains.

CASE STUDY
Data and AI strategy at a consumer product company

Data product domains

1 Sales and marketing:

   o Directly contributes to company OKR 1.

   o Scope: Europe across sales and marketing business divisions.

2 Customer support:

- o Directly contributes to company OKR 2.

- o Scope: North America and Europe across customer services divisions.

Formulating OKRs and milestones for the data product domains

Having selected data product domains that should be the focus of the data product strategy, objectives and key results for each data product domain need to be defined. There can also be several objectives under a data product domain. We recommend that the number of key results per objective should be limited to a maximum of five to ensure that the data product strategy is easy to read and understand for everyone in the organization. Objectives and key results should have metrics defined that make their contribution measurable.

CASE STUDY

Data and AI strategy at a consumer product company

OKRs for data product domains

Sales and marketing domain:

- Objective: Develop data products to increase customer loyalty and sales, and optimize pricing.

- Key results:

  - o Design one data product for optimizing pricing.

  - o Validate one data product for churn prediction.

  - o Deliver data product to increase cross- and up-sell opportunities by at least 5 per cent.

Customer support domain:

- Objective: Automate customer service by using natural language processing and algorithms to support customers directly or via customer service agents.

- Key results:

○ Ideate at least three data products to grow the level of support done on the website without call-centre agents.

○ Validate two data products to automatically formulate email responses.

○ Deliver data product to speed up onboarding for new customer care employees by two minutes.

Managing data products throughout their lifecycle

Every data product follows a lifecycle from ideation to retirement of the data product. Between each of the six lifecycle phases, a quality gate with defined checklists and responsibilities to sign off the quality gate ensures that all criteria have been met to continue with the next product phase. The design of data products starts with identifying data product ideas in the business domains of the data product strategy and prioritizing them based on business value, feasibility and contribution towards the overall strategy and vision. The best matching data product ideas are further defined from a product, business, user, feasibility and compliance perspective and some are filtered out if they cannot meet defined quality standards for one of these perspectives. Finally, the pre-filtered list of defined data product ideas is validated in a rapid prototyping process that aims to make ideas fail fast, so valuable resources are not wasted on ideas that do not work as hoped for. Creating great data product ideas is far from trivial as the effectiveness of data products has a high dependency on business processes and other software products used in a business domain, and the data that is available. The entire process is therefore like a big funnel where a lot of data product idea candidates come in at the top and become fewer and fewer with each step. At the same time, the likelihood rises with each step of a data product idea to actually work and have a sufficiently strong business impact. At the end of the process, the data product strategy can be revised and updated based on the learning and outcomes as new insights have been created.

The data product lifecycle has six phases overall:

1 **Ideating data products:** Ideas for data products need to be created and prioritized according to priorities set in the data product strategy.

2 **Designing data products:** Prioritized data product ideas are designed with regard to the product features, business value, target users, feasibility, ethics and compliance and further filtered based on a set of criteria.

3 **Validating data products:** Each remaining data product idea is validated using rapid prototyping and, if successful, prepared for development.

4 **Planning the delivery of data products:** Define the MVP further and plan development, deployment, operation and scaling.

5 **Developing and deploying data products:** Develop and document the data product in agile sprints and deploy it into production.

6 **Operating and scaling data products:** Run, support, expand and maintain the data product and scale it to further business scopes to increase value.

The delivery of a data product starts with the planning phase in which all aspects of the development, testing, deployment, operation, maintenance and scaling of the data product are thoroughly planned. Afterwards, the development and deployment phase during which the data product is implemented and documented as MVP using an agile approach in a series of development sprints. Moreover, testing and deployment ensure that the data product meets all quality standards and user expectations and create the foundation for the continuous development and integration of the data product after it goes live by establishing the deployment pipelines. At the end of this phase, the data product leaves the testing environment and goes live on the productive environment. In the final phase, the data product is operated and maintained in DevOps mode and scaled. This means that the responsibility for this phase lies with the same team that developed the data product. The scope of the data product is widened by adding more product features and by potentially adopting the data product to further user groups, eg by scaling the data product to other markets or production sites.

At some point during its lifetime, the decision might be taken that a data product is not needed any more or should be replaced with a new data product. Therefore, most data products sooner or later reach their end of life and are retired.

Monetizing data products

In some cases, data products can be monetized by selling them to third parties to generate a new data stream. The authors have observed several types of monetization. One is to sell quality assured raw data without much refinement. This could be, for example, raw sensor data collected by devices that capture weather conditions. The second related type of data monetization is to enrich data with further processing, refinement and advanced analytics. For instance, sensor data could be analysed to detect events that foresee changes in weather conditions. These new data points would be sold as enriched data. Both cases of selling raw and enriched data would be typical revenue streams for a data broker. It is important to ensure that there is a legal basis to sell data and that personal data protection is ensured and customer consent is given when necessary. A completely different type of monetization of data products is to sell not data, but AI services and algorithms. One way is to generate analytics models and algorithms with the data and providing them as a service. The consuming customer is using their own data following a similar schema to take advantage of the pre-trained models. An example could be a fraud detection algorithm that is provided to various banks as a service by a fintech company. Moreover, a different type of data monetization would be to generate an entirely new business service, for example to plan your travel journey, which is based on a number of data products that make the service smarter. Finally, data products might be the basis of a customer ecosystem, for which other companies might need to pay an access fee. The data product strategy is the basis for the further planning of the capability and technology and the transformation and culture strategies, which will be explained in the following sections.

Deriving the capability strategy

The capability strategy determines *which capabilities* we need to grow to succeed in data and AI. Organizational and technical capabilities are needed to actually deliver the data product strategy. Not adequately developing the required capabilities will simply mean not being able to deliver value. The capability strategy is the third pillar of your data and AI strategy. While the first two provide the general direction and focus on how to create business value with data and AI, the capability strategy looks at the organizational and technological aspects that are needed to be able to deliver the data products set out in the data product strategy and the strategy and vision. Data products need to run on a state-of-the-art agile data infrastructure and have to be operated, maintained and supported. Data pipelines have to be created to transport data from the source to the data lake and transform it into the right format to feed the machine learning algorithms as high-quality features. Data supplied to data products needs to be well understood and described in a data catalogue and the quality of the data has to be constantly monitored and, if necessary, improved. Legal and ethical aspects of data products need to be equally managed, which can be a very complex endeavour and oftentimes new unexplored territory. Reports, dashboards and self-service tools for business intelligence need to be provided for users in the business departments. Many data products require additional frontend and backend functionalities to be developed and all software components should be delivered through CI/CD pipelines (see Chapter 4) to ensure continuous integration and deployment without interfering with productive systems.

A capability strategy should include:

- defining the target picture for organizational and technical capabilities;
- assessing current capabilities to identify gaps in the target picture;
- developing objectives and key results for the capability strategy.

Defining the target picture for organizational and technical capabilities

Based on the priorities set out in the data product strategy, core capabilities need to be identified. A large set of capabilities are needed besides machine learning and data science to succeed in data and AI. The first step is therefore to create a target picture for the organizational set-up and the technical architecture. The target picture comprises all core capabilities that are necessary to implement the data product strategy.

CHECKLIST

Defining the target picture for capabilities, organization and technologies:

- identifying core capabilities for data and AI;
- defining roles and responsibilities;
- designing the organizational structure;
- developing processes and steering mechanisms;
- planning the data infrastructure and central data repositories;
- setting up the architecture and development standards for data products;
- creating the approach for data and AI governance.

Guidelines and best practices are discussed for the organizational aspects in Chapter 5 and for the technological aspects in Chapter 6. Each of the capabilities requires potential changes in the organization, business processes and the technology landscape. A justification for the value of the capability area can be given by stating which parts of the data product strategy the capability area is supporting.

CASE STUDY

Data and AI strategy at a consumer product company

Capability area: Machine learning and data science

- Capability definition: The ability to build, test, deploy and run high-quality machine learning and data science models.
- Impact on data product strategy: All data products that require machine learning models.

Capability area: Data infrastructure and operations

- Capability definition: The ability to build, test, deploy and run a state-of-the-art data and AI platform and to run, support and maintain data.

- Impact on data product strategy: All data products.

Assessing current capabilities to identify gaps in implementing the target picture

Next, including all business units in scope, we need to assess where we are today to identify the capabilities that still need to be developed to implement the target picture. Each capability in the existing organization is examined, and it is evaluated on a five-step scale of very low, low, medium, high and very high with regard to the maturity of this capability compared to the target picture. Gaps in implementing the target picture are identified and used as input to develop objectives and key results of the capability strategy.

CASE STUDY
Data and AI strategy at a consumer product company

Capability area: Machine learning and data science

- Current maturity assessment: Low.

- Achievements: First data scientists have been hired.

- Gap: So far, processes and quality gates for machine learning have not been established.

- Gap: Appropriate data science tools are missing.

Capability area: Data infrastructure and operations

- Current maturity assessment: Medium.

- Achievements: Cloud infrastructure and team initiated.

- Gap: Team and infrastructure are not yet fully up and running.

- Gap: Cloud and on-premise infrastructures are not interoperable.

Developing OKRs and milestones for the capability strategy

Objectives for the capability strategy should be based on the target picture and the assessment of the current state, with each goal focusing on one of these capabilities, further on called a capability area. The capability area should be further refined by formulating key results. Each capability area can have one or more metrics defined to track the success and maturity of the capability. Finally, milestones are defined, which, taken together, form the capability roadmap. Last, but not least, it is important to identify the resources required to implement the capability roadmap, which is usually a plan for the next quarters or years (depending on the planning horizon used in your company). A simple example of a part of a data and AI capability strategy is shown below.

CASE STUDY
Data and AI strategy at a consumer product company

Capability area: Machine learning and data science

- Objective: Build state-of-the-art machine learning and data science capabilities.
- Key results:
  o Year 1, Q2: New department for machine learning and data science set up.
  o Year 1, Q2: Adequate data science tools (eg Anaconda) introduced.
  o Year 2, Q2: Processes, standards and quality gates for machine learning and data science defined and implemented.
- Metrics:
  o High-quality machine learning and data science models deployed.

Capability area: Data infrastructure and operations

- Objective: Build state-of-the-art data infrastructure and operations.
- Key results:
  o Year 1, Q3: Data infrastructure and ops teams fully running.
  o Year 2, Q2: Interoperability of cloud and on-premise infrastructures ensured and data ops processes standardized and monitored.

- Metrics:
  - Security, reliability and agility metrics of the data platform.
  - Incident resolution time.
  - Number of incidents.

Developing the transformation strategy

The transformation strategy is the fourth pillar of your strategy and vision. The transformation strategy determines how the transformation of the company should be managed and how we can increase the willingness for change in the organization and create a data and AI driven culture. In the previous phases, we reinvented the corporate strategy and business vision, and defined a data product strategy and the strategy for building capabilities needed to deliver them. The transformation strategy looks now at the types of indispensable change activities that need to accompany the product delivery and capability building activities to make them successful and to build a data and AI driven culture. Moreover, the goals and milestones of the product, capability and transformation strategies are combined into a joint roadmap to implement the new corporate strategy and business vision. The joint transformation roadmap should be accompanied by an overarching view on goals and metrics that can be managed and tracked. This can be used to monitor the effectiveness of the implementation of the data and AI strategy. Without a transformation strategy you risk running into a lot of internal and external resistance by the staff and the stakeholders and a misalignment between data product strategy, capability strategy and the planned change management activities.

A transformation strategy for data and AI should involve:

- crafting the transformation story for your company's journey;
- identifying required change activities to implement strategy and vision;
- developing OKRs and milestones for change activities;

- harmonizing change activities with the data product strategy and capability strategy;
- designing the transformation roadmap and tracking its progress.

Crafting the transformation story for your company's journey

When driving digital transformation through data and AI, company leaders have to face many uncertainties and make big bets, which makes great storytelling crucial for the success of the transformation. Storytelling can be very powerful and sticky. Consequently, one of the first steps to undergo digital transformation and focus on data and AI is for the leadership to create and communicate a joint business vision and transformation story. The story should contain who we are today, what the steps in between are and what the realization of the business vision looks like. From the very beginning, it is a chance to set the right expectations of what stakeholders and employees can expect at what point in time. This way they see even small steps as the right step towards a bigger goal, which can be communicated as successes. The business vision and transformation story should not be reactive and solely based on pressure from the outside, for example with the statement 'We have to adopt digital transformation through data and AI because a competitor threatens our business model.' It should be based on a more positive and active approach, such as 'We aim to generate new income from the use of data and AI'.

The focus is on the revised corporate strategy and addresses how the business will react to transformation from the current business model to the new business model. Key steps of the transformation are formalized in the data and AI strategy with regard to data products, capabilities and change activities. Now, this overarching strategic goal has to be complemented with a clear statement on why this is important for the employees as well. The survival of the company forms the basis in the hierarchy of employee needs, but then there are further needs such as payment, promotion and new job opportunities within the company that should be addressed appropriately. Some will wonder if the new strategy and vision will require them to obtain training and include different tasks in their daily routine, others will be eager to explore whether there are new roles and opportunities available for them to advance in the organization. Many managers on all levels in traditional industries are anxious, as they do not feel sufficiently prepared and knowledgeable about data and AI and are afraid to lose management positions they worked for their entire life. At the beginning of the data and AI transformation process, the leadership may not have the answers to all of these questions, but they will have to communicate that they include them in their strategy and will provide updates on them as soon as they are available.

Categories of great innovation stories:[3]

- The 'best beats first' story is about the follower identifying opportunities that the competitor missed.
- The 'master of re-invention' story is about the courage of cannibalizing the core business.
- The 'serendipitous discovery' story is about having a eureka moment.
- The 'persistence' story is about hanging on even if it takes several tries.
- The 'unreasonable person' story is centred around a visionary person that leads the way.
- The 'winds of change' story is about recognizing the trends and acting accordingly.

Employees need to understand how data and AI should transform the organization and what their role in this transformation should be. A very effective method to do so is to show the relevant data, for example with this statement: 'Our projections show that if we do not undertake digital transformation in the next three years, we will lose 35 per cent of revenue and miss out on 28 per cent of cost cuttings. We will also lose our market share from 23 per cent to 12 per cent, because we will not have embraced the opportunities of new data products.' Once every employee has realized how important it is to make changes, they will be more willing to support the process.

Identifying the change activities that are required to implement the strategy and vision

There are many cultural challenges that need to be faced when driving digital transformation through data and AI. The change management aspect of implementing the reinvented corporate strategy and business vision, of growing capabilities and of implementing new data products at the heart of the organization is therefore worthy of special attention. CDOs have to ensure the changes are accompanied by adequate change management activities such as education and training, a communication plan and an adaptation of the incentive system.

Examples of cultural challenges for digital transformation through data and AI:

- Is there enough acceptance of important external stakeholders for digital transformation through data and AI and products, and can we improve it?

- How can we gain the support of employees for machine learning algorithms and data products developed for their work area?

- How can we increase the level of support of middle, upper and top management for data and AI?

- How open is IT and business to truly agile processes, modular software development and cloud platforms, and how can we widen support?

- What is the level of understanding and support from other business departments for data and AI, and how can it improve?

How much change management and transformation is called for really depends on the maturity and culture of the organization. In very data and AI driven organizations, sharing data across departments to automate a further core business processes might be not a big thing, as many other core business processes might have already gone through some of the change. But, even there, changes might affect some individuals more directly than others, and those should be taken care of. In less mature organizations, sharing data across departments and automating a core business process with machine learning can be a huge endeavour, as many things need to be set up at the same time and change could be perceived as threat.

CHECKLIST

Designing change management activities involves:

- assessing the current state of the data and AI culture to identify gaps;
- identifying incentives for staff and stakeholders to support the change;
- defining a training and education programme for staff and stakeholders;
- setting up a communication approach;
- planning the right amount of resources to implement the change activities.

A good first step is to understand the level of change demanded by the reinvented corporate strategy and business vision, the data product strategy and the capability strategy. Then, it makes sense to perform a quick assessment of the current data and AI culture across the business departments in the scope. It is often crucial to identify incentives to compensate staff and stakeholders that are negatively affected by the planned changes. For example, if certain manual tasks are not required anymore, managers should explain how the staff and stakeholders can play a role in the future, what is expected of them and how it will be made up for. Staff and stakeholders that require further or other skills would need to receive the right training and education opportunities. Moreover, an appropriate communication strategy has to be defined to communicate the changes that are ahead and what is required from and provided for the staff and the stakeholders. Ultimately, a transformation strategy roadmap needs to be created and required resources need to be allocated to support the implementation of the transformation strategy with the goal to create a win–win strategy for the CDO, the staff and the stakeholders.

Developing OKRs and milestones for change activities

Based on the need for change management, the objectives and key results including metrics should be defined for the change management activities as well. Each objective focuses on one particular aspect of the change programme. In our example below, the first objective focuses on education and skills, while the second objective aims to create incentives and compensation for employees and stakeholders to participate in the change process and to be more supportive and open towards the transformation required. Key results and associated metrics are tailored towards what each objective tries to achieve. In the first case, education and training work strives for a higher awareness and understanding of data and AI within the workforce, upper management and other stakeholders, and also to make employees fit for new or changed roles. In the second case, the key result is to reach as high a percentage as possible of employees and stakeholders that are affected by the change, with adequate incentives and compensation to increase the chance of getting more support to implement the changes. For all objectives and key results, the current state can be assessed as a baseline, and key milestones should also be defined.

CASE STUDY
Data and AI strategy at a consumer product company

Change activities

Change activity: Education and training

- Objective: Build skills and grow understanding for data and AI.
- Description: Create training and education opportunities to ensure that there is a broad understanding and acceptance of data and AI.
- Key results:
  o Basic understanding of data and AI for employees.
  o Basic understanding of data and AI for stakeholders.
  o Basic understanding of data and AI for top executives.
  o Further special training for employees to move into new roles and learn to operate adapted business processes through AI.
- Metrics:
  o Percentage of relevant employees, stakeholders and employees with higher data and AI awareness and understanding.

- o Number of employees trained for new roles and responsibilities and changed processes.
- Impact on product and capability strategies: All data products and capabilities are affected.
- Current maturity: Low.
- Milestones:
  - o Year 1, Q1: Foundation training for employees, stakeholders and executives completed.
  - o Year 2, Q3: Special training for employees completed.

Change activity: Incentives and compensation

- Objective: Create incentives for employees and stakeholders to support change.
- Description: Identify affected employees and stakeholders with a high risk of showing resistance to the implementation of the data and AI strategy and find appropriate ways to motivate them.
- Key results:
  - o Incentives for employees and stakeholders for supporting change in each data product domain.
  - o Incentives for employees and stakeholders to create understanding of and support for data and AI capabilities.
- Metrics:
  - o Percentage of employees incentivized to support changes in each data product domain and building data and AI capabilities.
  - o Percentage of stakeholders incentivized to support changes in each data product domain and building data and AI capabilities.
- Impact on product and capability strategies: All data products and capabilities affected.
- Current maturity: Medium.
- Milestones:
  - o Year 1, Q3: Incentive programme for employees set up.
  - o Year 2, Q4: Incentive programme for stakeholders set up.

Harmonizing change activities with the data product strategy
and capability strategy

The transformation roadmap determines when we plan to work with data and AI in the organization and combines the goals and milestones of all four perspectives (ie the strategy, product, capability and transformation perspectives) together in a joint roadmap. To be most effective, all perspectives should directly support each other. The transformation strategy therefore aims to integrate all three portfolios into a common roadmap that makes them consistent with each other. To begin with, it harmonizes the scopes between the data product domains, capability areas and change activities to ensure they are clearly overlapping and to fine-tune the planned activities, so they are supportive. If the data product strategy focuses on data products that require a lot of natural language processing, this should be reflected in the capability strategy. As always, timing is everything. If a change management activity comes too late, this might jeopardize the acceptance of the implementation of one or more critical data products. All resources that are needed to implement the product, capability and change roadmaps should be jointly planned, coordinated and approved to ensure that all three parts are truly supporting each other.

CHECKLIST

A transformation roadmap for data and AI should:

- ensure that the scope of each of the three strategies sufficiently overlap and support each other;
- harmonize the activities with regard to content and timing;
- create an overarching view on OKRs for data and AI;
- plan resources for implementing the entire data and AI strategy;
- track the implementation progress of the entire data and AI strategy.

Fundamentally, the heart of the corporate strategy and business vision is the company OKRs, as they determine why and what will be done with data and AI in the organization. As was previously mentioned, the capability strategy builds up capabilities that are needed to be able to deliver the data products of the data product strategy (see also Figure 2.2). There will be a large number of core capabilities that will be relevant for all the data product domains. Examples are developing and running the data and AI platform, the ability to deploy and run data products on the platform and the ability to manage data on the platform. Basic forms of machine learning, such as standardized approaches for supervised learning, might also be needed for all product domains, while more specific types of machine learning, such as voice and image recognition, will depend on the exact needs of the product domain. Similarly, the implementation of capabilities and data products will require support by employees and stakeholders and, thus, certain change activities will be needed to be able to succeed in implementation. Training experts in a business department might be required before they can understand and use the outputs of a machine learning algorithm that supports

FIGURE 2.2 The relationship between product, capability and transformation strategy

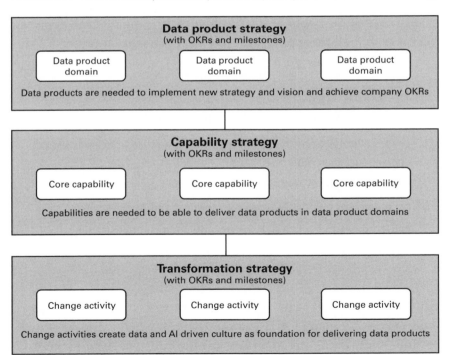

the automation of a core business process in the department. Taken altogether, milestones of the product domains will be dependent on milestones of the capability strategy and the transformation strategy, and these dependencies need to be considered when designing the transformation roadmap.

Designing the transformation roadmap and tracking its progress

When we design the transformation roadmap, a good starting point is to collect all milestones of the product, capability and transformation strategies into one common table, as illustrated in the case study, in which we have combined the examples of the consumer product company used earlier.

CASE STUDY
Data and AI strategy at a consumer product company

Milestones for data product strategy

Data product domain 1: Sales and marketing

- Data product milestone #P1.1: Go live of MVP for growing cross-sales of accessories matching main products → Planned for year 1, Q3.
- Data product milestone #P1.2: Go live of MVP for creating A/B testing experiments to examine pricing sensitivities for main products → Planned for year 2, Q3.

Etc...

Milestones for capability strategy

Capability area 1: Machine learning and data science

- Capability milestone #C1.1: New department for machine learning and data science set up. Adequate data science tools (eg Anaconda) introduced → Planned for year 1, Q2.
- Capability milestone #C1.2: Processes, standards and quality gates for machine learning and data science defined and implemented → Planned for year 2, Q2.

Etc...

Milestones for transformation strategy

Change activity 1: Education and training

- Transformation milestone #T1.1: Foundation training for employees, stakeholders and executives completed → Planned for year 1, Q1.
- Transformation milestone #T1.2: Special training for employees completed → Planned for year 2, Q3.

Etc...

As a next step, we identify dependencies between each of the milestones to understand which milestone needs to be moved because of a dependency. This can be done via a table that shows which milestones are interdependent, as shown in Table 2.1. If there is a dependency conflict, which means that one milestone A is dependent on a second milestone B but A is due before B is due, we need either to move milestone B to make it on time for milestone A if it is feasible and reasonable, or move milestone A to come after milestone B.

TABLE 2.1 An illustrative dependency list between milestones in a consumer goods company

	P1.1	P1.2	P2.1	P2.2	...
	depends on				
C1.1	●	●	●	●	
C1.2		●			
C2.1	●	●	●	●	
C2.2		●			
...					
T1.1	●	●	●	●	
T1.2				●	
...					

TABLE 2.2 A simplified transformation roadmap in a consumer goods company

	Year 1				Year 2			
	Q1	Q2	Q3	Q4	Q1	Q2	Q3	Q4
Product domain 1: Sales and marketing			●				●	
Product domain 2: Customer support						●		●
Etc...								
Capability area 1: Machine learning and data science		●				●		
Capability area 2: Data infrastructure and operations			●			●		
Etc...								
Change activity 1: Education and training	●						●	
Change activity 2: Incentives and compensation			●					●
Etc...								

Finally, all milestones can be shown in a transformation roadmap after conflicts between the milestones have been resolved, as illustrated in Table 2.2. This roadmap has considered all dependencies to ensure that the goals and targets of the data and AI strategy and transformation can be achieved.

The progress of the transformation can be tracked via the milestones defined and the achievements of OKRs as formulated when the product, capability and transformation strategies have been created.

Lessons learned and pitfalls for strategy and vision

Data product strategy leads, capabilities and change follow

What proportion of the data and AI budget should a company invest in products, capabilities or change? This is probably the biggest balancing act of the data and AI strategy. Strategy is all about finding the right trade-offs. A pitfall is to invest all in capabilities or change and not deliver any products. Another pitfall is to invest in capabilities and change activities that are not related to any products, as no synergies are created. Both can lead quickly to disappointment among the board and stakeholders as it becomes extremely difficult to show tangible results. A good practice is to align scopes and roadmaps of product, capability and transformation strategy to ensure that there are always some products that can be implemented early on and at every step of the journey and so that all capability and change activities directly provide benefits to product development and adoption.

Securing funding for the implementing of the data and AI strategy

Securing funding for the implementation of the entire data and AI strategy can be very challenging. The sum of investment could be simply too big to be used as one large chunk. To increase your chance of success, try finding areas that get a lot of executive attention and include them as main product domains in your data product strategy. How much funding is needed for implementing the data and AI strategy depends on three main factors:

1 The scope of the strategy.
2 The size of the product portfolio.
3 The current capabilities and culture available.

If you do not get sufficient budget to deliver the entire strategy, it is advisable to reduce the scope and the ambition level of the data product strategy to be able to deliver and to identify additional budget holders in the organizations that directly benefit from data products in a particular data product domain and approach them. It could well be that after implementing the first data products and capabilities, further budget holders will recognize the abilities of your team and admire the products you brought live and want to jump on the train. Then you could identify high-impact products in the domain of these admirers and secure the next small chunk of budget by adding them to your product portfolio. This is how you can grow step-by-step the overall size of your data and AI budget.

Closing the gap between strategy and reality

It is crucial to ensure that all activities you run are closely aligned with the data and AI strategy. Showing the value of the data and AI strategy requires a fast time to market of data products; therefore, do not oversize the MVP you build. It is easier to expand the feature scope once products are live rather than having an endless development phase for the first product. Create a limit for the number of data products per domain and look for synergies to ensure that delivery is possible. Start planning for production and scaling early on, as online live and scaled products create substantial and visible business value. Most often, business processes need to be changed to adopt data products. Create cross-functional teams involving those people who will be affected in the business departments that will be using the data products to automate their tasks. This will lead to better products that can actually solve real business problems, and increase the willingness of people in the department to change the business processes as required and to use the data product.

Template for a transformation roadmap

Table 2.3 can be used as a template to describe and visualize all the milestones of the digital transformation through data and AI.

TABLE 2.3 Template for milestone tracking of transformation roadmap

	Year 1				Year 2			
	Q1	Q2	Q3	Q4	Q1	Q2	Q3	Q4
Data product strategy								
Product domain 1:								
Product domain 2:								
Product domain 3:								
Product domain 4:								
Capability strategy								
Capability area 1:								
Capability area 2:								
Capability area 3:								
Capability area 4:								
Transformation strategy								
Transformation activity 1:								
Transformation activity 2:								
Transformation activity 3:								
Transformation activity 4:								

Summary and conclusion

At the heart of data and AI transformation is the new strategy and vision. It redefines the current business model, the corporate strategy and business vision, sets the priorities for the data product portfolio and for capabilities and technologies that have to be built, and integrates everything into a joint transformation roadmap supplemented by appropriate change management activities. The data product strategy defines the data product domains and metrics that should be tackled by data products; however, it does not prescribe exactly which data products should be built. This is done in the data product design phase, which is covered in the next chapter.

Notes

1 Chui, M, *et al*, Notes from the AI frontier: Applications and value of deep learning, McKinsey Global Institute Discussion Paper, April 2018

2 Chui, M, *et al*, Notes from the AI frontier: Applications and value of deep learning, McKinsey Global Institute Discussion Paper, April 2018

3 Birkinshaw, J, Telling a good innovation story: Appealing to people's emotions helps new ideas cut through the clutter, *McKinsey Quarterly*, 3, (July 2018), pp 8–12

03

Data product design

LEARNING OBJECTIVES FOR THIS CHAPTER
- Learn how to create great data product ideas in the data product domains.
- Learn how to design new data products involving users.
- Learn how to validate new data products and test their feasibility.
- Learn about the relationship between strategy and data product design.
- Learn to reuse as much as possible in product design to save time.
- Learn how to choose the right participants for data product ideation.

Key principles for designing data products

The product strategy sets the focus for where data and AI products will contribute to the company's success. In this chapter, it is all about designing data products to implement the data product strategy. Learning from failed data product ideas can be as important as those ideas that succeed as long as it is used as an opportunity to reflect and revise the goals in the data product strategy and to adjust the portfolio.

The strategy and vision have highlighted data product domains and goals. Now, data product ideas need to be identified and then designed and validated, ideally to directly support the implementation of the strategy and vision. An initial machine learning model prototype is developed to prove feasibility.

FIGURE 3.1 The three phases of designing data products

The design of data products follows three phases:

1 **Ideating data products:** Ideas for data products need to be created and prioritized according to priorities set in the data product strategy.

2 **Designing data products:** Prioritized data product ideas are designed with regard to the product features, business value, target users, feasibility, ethics and compliance, and further filtered based on a set of criteria.

3 **Validating data products:** Each remaining data product idea is validated using rapid prototyping and, if successful, prepared for development.

Key principles for ideating data products

The first part of the data product design process is to run ideation workshops in the core data product domains of the strategy and vision to create ideas for new data products and to prioritize among them. Each data product idea can then be evaluated in terms of feasibility and business impact. The scores for feasibility and business impact are the basis for prioritizing which data products are allowed to continue to the product design phase.

KEY PRINCIPLES
Data product ideation

• Ideation is focused on the data product domains of the data product strategy.

• Representative business stakeholders and users in each of the data product domains are selected to participate in the ideation workshops.

- Ideation workshops aim to educate, inspire and empower the participants so they can come up with great data product ideas.
- Each data product idea is evaluated in terms of impact and feasibility.
- The best data product ideas are chosen for validation.

Key principles for designing data products

Those data product ideas that have been prioritized during the data product ideation phase continue to the data product design phase. A data product idea has to be properly described and defined and further evaluated before it makes sense to start the validation. Otherwise, we might waste time by validating a data product that has not been adequately thought through. We might not know what is actually evaluated or we may validate something that is not feasible, has no value or is not allowed. Based on the authors' experience, it is advisable to define every data product from five different perspectives:

1 Product perspective.

2 Business perspective.

3 User perspective.

4 Feasibility perspective.

5 Compliance perspective.

If all five perspectives are clearly defined and fulfil the set criteria, the data product can enter the data product validation phase.

KEY PRINCIPLES
Data product design

- The data product should have a clearly defined set of product features.
- Each data product has a business impact measured with the metrics for the respective data product domain and ideally an engaged business sponsor.

- Future users of the data product are known and the user experience is designed in a way that matches their needs.
- There is a solution architecture design for the data product, which explains how it can be built with the technologies and data available.
- Legal, regulatory and ethical challenges can be addressed appropriately.

Key principles for validating data products

Data products that have been fully defined and can meet the requirements from a product, business, user, technical and compliance perspective enter the data product validation phase. For each of the five perspectives, there can be aspects that are quite uncertain. The goal of the validation phase is to examine these aspects and test them as fast as possible. For example, if the technical feasibility of a machine learning model is unclear, a proof of concept could assist in establishing if the data is good enough to create a high-quality machine learning model. The aim of the validation phase is to reduce uncertainties with regard to the design and evaluation of the data product. The goal at this stage is not to build a working data product.

KEY PRINCIPLES
Validating data products

- A prototype of the data product is created with as little effort as possible.
- The business impact is verified through the prototype.
- The acceptance and expectations of the users are tested.
- The technical and machine learning feasibility is validated with real data.
- Legal, ethical and other compliance issues are investigated.

The following sections describe practical methodologies and good practices for each phase. We start with the data product ideation phase.

Ideating data products

The goal of the data product ideation phase is to generate a wide range of different data product ideas in the data product domains of the data product strategy, with participants that can represent these domains well and that receive an introductory session about data products. While quality is more important than quantity of ideas, often some of the best data product ideas are not the obvious ones and therefore blue ocean thinking should be allowed at this stage. The evaluation of feasibility and business impact can only be a rough estimate based on expert judgement and crowd wisdom, as there will usually be a lot of data product ideas to evaluate at this stage of the process. A more formal evaluation of feasibility and business impact is conducted later on during the data product design phase for those data products that qualify for the next phase. The outcome of the data product ideation phase is a list of selected top data product ideas based on the ranking, preferences and priorities of the business stakeholders. For these top ideas, a team is defined that will be involved in the data product design phase. There are four steps in the data product ideation phase.

STEPS IN THE DATA PRODUCT IDEATION PHASE

1   Choosing the focus and participants for the data product ideation.

2   Inspiring and educating participants to start a data product ideation.

3   Creating and clustering a wide range of different data product ideas.

4   Evaluating and prioritizing data product ideas and selecting the team for the data product design phase.

Choosing the focus and participants for the data ideation phase

The choice of participants during the ideation phase depends on a number of factors. First of all, there is the question of which data product domains should be in focus. If the selected domain for a product ideation phase is, for example, sales and marketing, then the selected participants should be experts in this data product domain. It is recommended that one data product domain is focused on at a time to keep the amount of incoming data product ideas and stakeholders manageable. It is possible to run a data product ideation phase for all data product domains at the same time as part of a larger project to create the data and AI strategy for the first time. This requires, of course, much more capacity than tackling one domain after the other. Within one data product domain, there can be many different subdomains, eg brand management could be one subdomain within sales and marketing. It is possible to limit the ideation phase to some selected subdomains in which finding promising ideas for data products is more likely. For each subdomain in scope, there should preferably be at least two participants chosen that represent the subdomain during the data product ideation phase. Inviting senior stakeholders of the product domain to some of the data product ideation workshops has the major advantage that the process is more transparent to them and they can bring in their own ideas and influence the prioritization of required features, which often results in increased management support and engagement in the next phases. The facilitators of data product ideation workshops can be data product managers and data scientists (see pages 145–151 for role descriptions), preferably with some knowledge of the respective data product domain, which can ensure that the ideation phase is executed properly and that ideation participants have a sparring partner with a lot of expertise in data and AI to consult with.

CHOOSING THE FOCUS AND PARTICIPANTS

1 Focus on one data product domain at a time.

2 Identify the subdomains that should be in scope of the ideation.

3 Choose at least two participants for each of the subdomains in scope.

4 Invite senior stakeholders to some of the ideation sessions to obtain buy-in.

5 Provide facilitators with a data and AI background to run the ideation phase.

Inspiring and educating participants to start a data product ideation

A vital step during the data product ideation phase is for participants to receive inspirational training on data and AI. This should be at least a one-hour session, but could be an extended training session that runs for several days. The content of these training sessions should focus on understanding fundamental concepts of data and AI such as, for example, data architecture and management, and supervised and unsupervised machine learning. Moreover, concrete examples for data products inside and outside the organization should be provided to make the concepts more tangible and demonstrate how they can be applied in practice. This can be supplemented by giving insight into the work of a data scientist; for example, how data is prepared, how features are engineered and how machine learning models are built, tested and deployed. Finally, the data product lifecycle phase should be explained to prepare the participants for the next steps after ideating, ie validating, developing, deploying, operating and scaling a data product. The result of the training sessions is that participants can better understand when and how data and AI can generate value, and how to unlock it. The inspirational and educational sessions can be integrated into the first part of an ideation workshop as a warm-up before the actual data product ideation takes place. They should conclude with an opportunity for participants to ask any open questions to data and AI experts.

DATA PRODUCT INSPIRATION AND EDUCATION WORKSHOP

- Introduce fundamental concepts of data and AI to participants.
- Give concrete examples for data products to inspire participants.
- Provide insights into the practical work of data scientists.
- Explain the data product lifecycle.
- Run a question and answers session with data and AI experts.

Creating and clustering a wide range of different data product ideas

After having inspired and educated the participants, the actual ideation workshops take place for each data product subdomain. If the number of representatives for each subdomain is small, it can make sense to have participants from several subdomains in only one workshop. The data product ideation workshop starts with every workshop participant writing up their ideas for new data products or enhancements of existing data products. This is a silent exercise to ensure that everyone can write up their own ideas independently. Each idea should be written on a separate post-it note with a short title, what data could potentially be used, the algorithm or data processing likely to be needed and the action and impact that could result from the data product being in place. Afterwards, each data product idea is presented to all workshop participants by reading out the title and explaining the basic idea behind the data product. The data product ideas can be clustered into themes, and if a data product idea is very similar to another one they can be combined into one idea and could then represent different features of the same data product idea.

DATA PRODUCT IDEATION WORKSHOP

1 Workshop participants write up their ideas on post-it notes, one idea per post-it and on their own.

2 Each data product idea is described on paper (see below).

3 Every participant explains their ideas and puts them into a new or existing data product cluster.

A data product idea should be described as follows:

- Title: A short title for the data product.
- Data: The data needed to implement the data product.
- Algorithm: The data processing or algorithms required.
- Action: How the data product is used and creates business impact.

Evaluating and prioritizing data product ideas and selecting the planning team

After ideating data product ideas, they are evaluated and prioritized during a second workshop. The first dimension is impact, which refers to how much business value can potentially be generated by the data product, for example in terms of strategic importance, increase in profitability and customer loyalty, reduction in cost and risk or improvement of other metrics relevant in the data product domain. The second dimension is feasibility and reflects how easily the data product can be implemented considering all possible implementation difficulties such as, for example, technical aspects, cultural resistance, required business process changes, needed involvement of external and internal stakeholders, compliance challenges and any other relevant aspects. Each data product idea is evaluated on a scale from 1 to 5, with 1 being the lowest score and 5 being the highest score in two dimensions.

EVALUATION AND PRIORITIZATION WORKSHOP

1 Each data product idea is evaluated with regard to feasibility and business impact.

2 The scoring can be used to put the product idea on a graph with an impact on the x-axis and feasibility on the y-axis.

3 A ranking is created based on the average score and then calibrated. For example, if it is discovered that a data product idea is much more feasible than another then the score should be adapted accordingly to reflect the high feasibility.

4 Data product ideas that have an average score of at least 4 are pre-selected. The group decide which best-ranked data product ideas to prioritize.

5 Each data product that should be continued is prepared for the data product design phase and a team is selected for the next phase.

The evaluation of a data product is done at this stage along two dimensions:

- Feasibility: The amount of effort needed to implement the data product (scale 1 to 5).

- Impact: The level of potential business benefit that will be created (scale 1 to 5).

The scale ranges from 1 'very low', 2 'low', 3 'medium', 4 'high' to 5 'very high'.

Every data product idea can be now provided with a unique number and placed as a point with that number on a graph that shows the impact score on the x-axis and the feasibility score on the y-axis. In this way, there is a simple visual that shows the top-scoring data products that will facilitate further discussion. A ranked order of evaluated ideas can be created based on the two scores. The ranking and scores need to be calibrated to ensure that ideas with the same score are comparable with regard to their expected feasibility and impact. Based on the calibrated scoring and ranking of ideas, a filtered ranked list is created with all those that have a minimum average score of 3.5. If there are more than 10 ideas left for the data product subdomain, the minimum average score of impact and feasibility can be increased to 4 or even higher to filter out ideas with a lower impact and feasibility. The ideas that have been filtered out are parked in a data product ideas backlog. The workshop participants and senior stakeholders select the most popular idea from the top five, and this is prioritized in the design phase. A team is recruited from relevant business departments and a data product manager is nominated who takes ownership of the selected idea during the design and validation phases, which will be covered next.

CASE STUDY
Data product ideation at a consumer goods company

1 Data product: Grow cross-sales of accessories matching main products.

   o Sub-goal: Create more cross- and up-sell opportunities.

   o Impact: High.

- o   Feasibility: High.
- o   Pilot scope: Headphones.
- o   Milestones: MVP go live in year 1, Q3, 'quick win'.
- o   → Potential scaling to be determined after pilot.
- o   Quick win!

2   Data product: Create A/B testing experiments to examine pricing sensitivities for main products.
- o   Sub-goal: Optimize pricing for consumer products.
- o   Impact: Very high.
- o   Feasibility: Medium.
- o   Pilot scope: Headsets, PC Speakers.
- o   Milestones: MVP go live in year 2, Q3.
- o   → Potential scaling to be determined after pilot.

3   Data product: Create optimal product bundles.
- o   Sub-goal: Create more cross- and up-sell opportunities.
- o   Impact: High.
- o   Feasibility: Medium.
- o   Pilot scope: All audio products.
- o   Milestones: MVP go live in year 3, Q1.
- o   → Potential scaling to be determined after pilot.

4   Data product: Analyse which items are bought together.
- o   Sub-goal: Create more cross- and up-sell opportunities.
- o   Impact: Medium.
- o   Feasibility: High.
- o   Pilot scope: All audio products.
- o   Milestones: MVP go live in year 3, Q2.
- o   → Potential scaling to be determined after pilot.

5   Data product: Assess reasons why customers change to competition.
- o   Sub-goal: Increase customer loyalty and reduce churn.
- o   Impact: Medium.
- o   Feasibility: Low.
- o   Milestones: None due to low feasibility.

Designing data products

Throughout the data product ideation phase, a variety of data product ideas have been discovered, evaluated and prioritized. Now some data product ideas have qualified in each data product domain to enter the data product design phase. In this phase, the data product team will jointly define the data product they are in charge of. It starts with a refinement of the problem statement. This statement simply contains the business problem that should be solved with the respective data product. Moreover, the data product is evaluated and described along five distinct perspectives.

The design of data products is done from five different perspectives:

1 The **product perspective** defines what the data product does and how it works.

2 The **business perspective** identifies and calculates the potential business impact of the data product, compares it to the expected implementation costs and determines the most relevant business stakeholders for the data product.

3 The **user perspective** defines the user experience and how the data product will be integrated into the daily workflow of the business users, including how business processes will be adapted if necessary.

4 The **feasibility perspective** examines the technical feasibility and the availability of data of sufficient quality.

5 The **compliance perspective** investigates whether the data product requires any legal and compliance approvals and the likelihood of obtaining them. It also looks at legal, compliance and ethical barriers for data product implementation.

The data product design phase is facilitated by the responsible data product manager and supported by the data product team that was put together at the end of the ideation phase. All five perspectives, taken together, define the data product and show what it does, if it is economically and technically feasible, if users would accept it and if it is legal, compliant and ethically desirable. Each of these perspectives can provide a good reason not to continue with the data product into the product validation phase. In contrast, a positive evaluation from all five perspectives provides a solid starting point for entering the next phase.

The product perspective

The product perspective defines what the data product does and how it does it, in particular the functionalities of the data product and the design of the interface to the user or to other systems.

DESIGNING PRODUCT FEATURES

The core of a data product is actually defined by the set of product features that the data product should contain to deliver the expected functionalities that lead to the desired business impact and user experience. Following the agile principles, it makes sense to limit the amount of product features to be built into the first iteration of the data product, to ensure fast implementation and testing in a real-life environment. Therefore, a minimum viable product (MVP) should be defined, which contains the core set of product features needed to bring a data product live that can solve the business problem it is designed for to a significant degree, while not including product features that can be added at a later stage. These initial product features should be sufficient to satisfy early user needs. Note that product features should not be confused with the features of a machine learning model (which is the processed and transformed data to be used as an input parameter to a machine learning model).

FORMULATING THE INTERFACE DESIGN REQUIREMENTS

In general, there are two different types of interfaces for a data product: an API receives settings from and provides the result to a different IT system, while a user interface receives settings and provides the results in a visualized form to a human user. In many cases, a data product has both types of interfaces at the same time. In the first case, consuming IT systems for the API need to be described, including their requirements. In the second case, a user frontend needs to be designed, which needs to consider the user perspective.

The business perspective

This perspective looks at the economic side of things and aims to identify business stakeholders that benefit from the data product, to assess the business impact and to calculate the business case of the data product by contrasting the economic gains with the efforts to develop, deploy, operate and maintain the data product.

IDENTIFYING RELEVANT BUSINESS STAKEHOLDERS

There are many reasons why it is important to identify senior business stakeholders that become business owners, sponsors or co-sponsors for a data product. If nobody owns a data product then one could assume that nobody believes in its value and the question arises of why one should bother to build it in the first place. Vice versa, if there are many senior business stakeholders that show a deep interest in a data product, it is apparent that there must be some value in it. So the right question to ask is: Who will benefit the most from the data product inside the organization? It has to be answered and is often not that trivial. The most obvious way is to approach business stakeholders that have demonstrated their interest in the data product during the ideation phase. Oftentimes, data products that automate business processes do not attract much interest from the leaders of teams that would lose part of their tasks if they were automated. In such cases, the relevant business stakeholders might be the more senior managers that they report to. If all the benefits are distributed among many internal business stakeholders, it can be especially difficult to determine who can be a sponsor. In such cases, if the data product has a high business impact the right sponsor could be the management board or top executives, who have a wider interest in the firm in their scope of work.

ASSESSING THE BUSINESS IMPACT OF A DATA PRODUCT

The main rationale for why a data product is important to an organization is its business impact. Therefore, a crucial part of designing a data product is to investigate the ways the data product can affect business outcomes measured by the metrics in the respective data product domain, and its contribution to strategy and vision. This needs to be supplemented with a logical argumentation and reasonable estimates for the numbers that quantify the impact. There are many types of business impacts. Some examples are:

- increased efficiency (eg reduction in the number of working hours);
- improved decision-making (quality);
- improved customer satisfaction (eg conversion);
- improved employee satisfaction (eg lower fluctuation);
- entering a new market (new customers);
- enabling a new business model (eg a new value proposition).

In the product design phase, a decision on which business impact a product generates and a rough estimate on its magnitude is needed to obtain buy-in to move to the product validation phase.

The user perspective

During the product design process it is tempting to focus on the desired business outcome or the business problem that should be solved with the particular product. While it is important to keep the overall goal of the product in mind, the user should be at the centre of the actual product design. Setting the personas and user journeys builds a solid foundation to start with the more detailed product design, which lays out the user interface. Simple exercises, such as imagining the user not as an abstract concept but as a person with specific characteristics, can help with that. The user experience (UX) refers to every single interaction a user has with the data product. Reflecting on and visualizing these interactions as part of the user journey allows the UX to be refined and enhanced. The product design process could directly involve users to co-create the product design and conduct user testing to get feedback on initial product designs.

CREATING PERSONAS

Creating user personas can be conducted as a team brainstorming exercise that enables the team to put themselves in the user's shoes and to develop a common understanding on who the user is and what they want from the product. First, the team makes assumptions on the user's background that are relevant for the product (eg project manager in a startup). Second, they write down the problems that they expect the user to have (eg manifold concurrent tasks that are difficult to keep track of). Third, they map these problems to the solutions that the product should have (eg project management tool that helps monitor and prioritize different tasks). This initial brainstorming exercise should be validated by research to ensure that the defined personas actually correspond to reality.

CREATING USER JOURNEYS

For each created persona, there should be a user journey that describes each interaction the persona has with the product. The user journey should include the touchpoints, actions, thoughts and emotions for each persona while they use the product. Touchpoints refer to any channels or media which enable a persona to interact with the product, such as social media or online ads, as well as product elements that the persona uses, such as the login button, the ordering menu or purchasing menu. Actions include all the activities that a persona conducts in the tool, such as logging in, ordering a t-shirt, and purchasing that t-shirt. Considering the thoughts and emotions a user experiences while interacting with a product makes it possible to reflect more deeply on how to improve the user experience. For example, if the emotion after ordering a t-shirt with the help of the product is 'I am so happy I bought that t-shirt!' a product designer will consider, depending on the target audience, if it might be useful to include a user interface element that reflects that emotion, such as a playful detail in the form of a smiley or heart as part of a button to complete the transaction.

The feasibility perspective

The feasibility perspective defines the requirements for data transformation and algorithm design, the data needed and data sources available, and an initial draft of a solution architecture for the data product. This can involve getting the first data extracts and starting to check the data suitability for the data product to quickly evaluate its general feasibility.

IDENTIFYING DATA REQUIREMENTS AND DATA SOURCES

The biggest showstopper for data products is the unavailability of appropriate data needed to implement the data product. The following questions serve as starting point for a gap analysis for this issue and can be used to estimate the effort needed to obtain and use the appropriate data:

1 What kind of data do we need for the data product?

2 What kind of data is available? Data catalogues often do not exist. Interviews with data experts in the relevant data product domains are a good approach.

3 What quality does the data have? The first step is to obtain data extracts to examine the usefulness of the data.

DESIGNING THE INITIAL SOLUTION ARCHITECTURE

Most data products, once they are operated and used in a productive environment, rely on getting data from other systems and providing data to other systems. As part of the data product design, an initial solution architecture should, therefore, be defined by following these questions:

1 Which systems need to send which data and how often?

2 Which systems need to receive and process which data and how often?

3 With which operational frontend applications would we need to integrate? Is an adaptation of the frontend needed or should we design it from scratch?

This can be visualized in a context diagram by showing which applications feed into the data product and which applications receive data from the data product.

The compliance perspective

The compliance perspective ensures that data products comply with laws and regulations, and that ethical standards are set and followed.

Laws, regulations and ethics can differ a lot between geographies, therefore the local context needs to be considered and adapted while maintaining the global compliance and ethical rules of the organization set in the headquarters. Step by step, every potential legal, regulatory and ethical concern needs to be defined and examined.

DEFINING THE COMPLIANCE PERSPECTIVE

Identifying legal and regulatory requirements and barriers

There is a multitude of national and international laws that need to be observed. In particular, data privacy laws, most prominently the GDPR in the European Union, tightly restrict how data and AI can be used in practice and often provide a strict framework that must be implemented. The collection and use of personal data has to be concise and clear. There are many more legal requirements resulting from, for example, contracts, antitrust law, intellectual property law. Moreover, depending on which industry the organization is in, industry-specific regulations might apply, for example in the financial industry (eg Basel III) and in the pharmaceutical industry (eg FDA Code of Federal Regulations).

Identifying ethical requirements and barriers

While laws and regulations provide quite strict boundaries, ethical aspects of data and AI are much less clear. In a way, here the company needs to position themselves with regard to their customers, stakeholders, employees, the environment, the local community and society in general. Unethical behaviour can in extreme cases be really bad for the business, as customers and stakeholders might turn away from the company and its products. As an important part of data product design, ethical concerns with regard to the data product should be identified and evaluated. Two major aspects to evaluate are the purpose of the data product and its technical robustness. It makes sense to continue with the validation of the data product only if the evaluation concludes that it is ethically justifiable based on the values of the organization and its employees. The European Commission's High-Level Expert Group on Artificial Intelligence (AI HLEG) have defined ethical guidelines and policy and investment recommendations that can be used as a good starting point to define the data and AI ethics framework in your organization.[1]

After the data product has been defined from each of the five perspectives, a decision must be made on whether the data product can or should continue to the data product validation phase. Any data product entering the data product validation phase should have a high impact for the business, be desired by the users and be feasible and compliant.

Validating data products

Data products coming successfully through the product design phase move on to the data product validation phase. All five perspectives from the product design phase are re-assessed and validated through rapid prototyping and further examination.

Rapid prototyping

It is important to quickly build a prototype that can be tested, both in terms of the quality of the model and the user experience. It is better to build a prototype of the data product fast and possibly determine after the validation phase to cease investing in it, rather than spending a long time developing the MVP and discovering that it cannot be used after all. For this, it helps to quickly build a wireframe or conceptual prototype that can be shown to potential users and business stakeholders to ask for their feedback and gain their buy-in. More often than not, more senior business stakeholders find a conceptual prototype and a vision for the product for the next couple of years more appealing than a problem statement tailored to the needs of a small group of users. Additionally, some compliance issues can require more thorough preparation and assessment including open source documentation, data protection and information security considerations, as well as alignment with the company's specific legal requirements and branding guidelines. These issues should be assessed and planned before entering the product delivery planning phase, not least because the specialists in charge of these topics are usually in high demand.

Sketching the user journey with mock-ups and wireframes

User interface (UI) elements comprise the parts of a data product that are visible to the user and which enable the user to interact with a product. They can be broadly classified into input, navigation and information elements. The following list contains examples for each UI element type:

- Input elements: eg button, drop-down list, checkbox, date and time picker, text field, stepper, toggle switch.
- Navigation elements: eg navigation bar, sidebar, icon, search field, pagination.
- Information elements: eg progress bar, modal, tool-tip, notification.

A design system encompasses brand guidelines, asset libraries and documentation with exact specifications for all UI elements, that is, which fonts, font sizes, colours, shapes and styles to apply for buttons, navigation bars, etc. These specifications are essentially ready-to-use code for all UI elements and therefore allow quick prototyping. A design system ensures that a company or brand has a consistent layout that is easily recognizable and conveys the brand vision. Many design systems grant a certain degree of flexibility, so that, for example, the product designer picks a colour from a range of suggestions and uses the corresponding colour palette for the UI. Designing a product should be regarded as a major part of a team's development process. Naturally, a product designer will take the lead in this process, but the whole team should actively participate to ensure that the design aligns with the product vision and user story mapping. At the beginning of a product development process or when new features are added to a product it often helps to ask every team member and a number of potential users to contribute to the product design by drawing and presenting their own sketch of the most important product features. This allows the different perspectives to be incorporated and provides a fruitful starting point for discussions. The sketches arising as consensus from these discussions can then be used as templates for mock-ups or wireframes that represent a more formalized and polished look and feel of the product, which can serve as a basis of decision-making for business stakeholders. The wireframe shows how the different views of the tool are going to come out, including the most important features and UI elements. Clickable wireframes enable the user to simulate what a real interaction with the tool would be like and might even serve as a conceptual prototype which can also be used for user testing to obtain feedback on a product before the actual product development has started.

Finding, understanding and evaluating data

An important part of data product validation, the input data for the machine learning models and data transformations, needs to be gathered as a one-time extract from the different IT source systems. This can be a cumbersome task as it is often not straightforward to find the data needed for the data product and approvals are usually required to get data access. Once the data is available, it needs to be understood. If there is a data catalogue in place that describes the data, this might be an easy task. Otherwise, interviewing subject matter experts from different business and IT departments will be the best way to find out more about the content of the data. A first data profiling can also help get a better understanding of the contents of the datasets. Data usually needs to be processed and cleansed to make it ready for the data transformations and machine learning model training that form the data product. In more advanced set-ups, requirements can also define the necessary input and output data quality checks to verify the validity of the results.

Validating the data science and machine learning approach

At the heart of a data product, data is transformed and algorithms are applied to the input data. An important step is to define the features and the target variable for the machine learning model. Moreover, minimum quality criteria need to be defined for the model, which means how well the model needs to be able to predict. This depends a lot on how the data product is supposed to be used and how much damage it can do if a prediction goes wrong. The features that can be used for training the machine learning model need to be computed based on the input data. Data is then divided into a training set and a test set. As part of the data product validation phase, different machine learning model archetypes (eg decision trees, random forests, neural networks, linear regressions) are applied to the training data to train a model. The supervised models are subsequently evaluated using the test data and compared with the minimum required model quality for the data product. If no model can fulfil the set quality criteria for the data product, further features can be generated and other models can be tested. After a few circles, at some point, the decision has to be made about whether the machine learning model is good enough for the data product. If not, this might be a main reason not to continue with the data product. If it is, three parts need to be investigated to prepare the MVP: the data input, the data processing and the data output. More detailed requirements can include how often data needs to be refreshed, how frequent the model needs to be run once it is deployed, how fast output needs to be delivered and how frequently a trained model needs to be retrained with new data.

Verifying the business impact and building the business case

For the validation phase, the value proposition is defined more clearly and the business impact is quantified. For the value proposition, it is important to be responsive to any underlying reservations and cultural restraints. Many data products enable the automation of business processes. This can have the consequence that business processes require less manual effort, deliver more consistent results, run faster and smoother, are available 24 hours a day or produce a higher quality of results. These types of impacts are particularly hard to accept, as human work needs to be compared to machine work, which can be a politically difficult endeavour. Subject matter experts that are currently involved or in charge of a business process that can be potentially automated might cast doubt on the quality of the machine output to undermine the estimated business impact reasoning. If baselines and measurement metrics are clearly defined, business process automation through data products can be benchmarked against the existing manual labour intensive approach by running both approaches in parallel and by simply comparing the numbers to provide evidence for the estimated business impact. Another type of business impact is that data products improve decision-making by providing additional insight. This type of impact is particularly hard to prove in practice unless the decision is fully automated, as human decision-makers are usually the ones consuming the insight. It can be difficult to collect evidence directly for this type of impact and one often has to rely on the arguments of human decision-makers who can say that the data product has the potential to improve decision-making by x per cent and can provide a justification for the estimated business impact (eg more insights into customer segments allow for more targeted marketing campaigns). Finally, for some data products the estimation and measurement of business impact can be fairly simple. For example, in a digital and direct marketing environment, one can simply count the increased number of conversions or leads generated through a data product that runs algorithms to automate the engagement mechanisms with different target audiences.

The business case for a data product should calculate the estimated business impact generated by the data product over time and subtract the estimated effort to build, run and maintain the data product. The effort to create and operate the data product should be based on the assumptions made from the product and feasibility perspectives. The time horizon of the business case is usually set between three and five years after the investment has been made and depends on the financial controlling guidelines in the organization.

Early user testing

User testing sessions serve as crucial milestones for product validation and should be included as such in the product roadmap from early on, irrespective of exactly which features can be shown by then. It is important to include user feedback at an early stage. This has several advantages. First, setting fixed dates for user testing sessions helps focus on the user perspective even before the actual product development starts. Second, user testing sessions can be used to obtain feedback on a number of essential product features, so that countermeasures can be taken quickly if the users feel that the product has developed in the wrong direction. Third, it can recruit advocates for the product who are willing to vouch for it and might serve as early adopters. For data products, it is very important as part of the user testing to allow the user to test and verify the machine learning model prototype and ask if they are satisfied with the performance and whether it behaves as expected.

DESIGNING AND CONDUCTING USER TESTING SESSIONS

Adherence to the following principles has proven valuable for user testing sessions:

- Recruit participants with distinct roles and from a variety of departments to obtain feedback from different user perspectives.

- Send the invitations early to ensure that senior users can participate and avoid frantic last-minute searches for alternatives.

- Allow the user to test the product on their own, while providing them with minimal guidance. This reveals whether the product works intuitively or if it needs additional informative elements or redesign.

- Watch the user closely while they work with the tool and take notes on at which points they hesitate. Ask them to share their thoughts while using the tool, and what they would improve in terms of design, content and usability.

- Set up a formal written feedback system, including fixed questions, metrics and free comment fields. This feedback system can be reused in the next user testing sessions to monitor progress in user satisfaction.

- Incorporate workshop elements into the user testing session to establish a direct interaction with the users and increase their involvement in the product. Examples include short discussions on the details of a future feature or a brainstorming exercise on how the product could be applied in other contexts.

- Wrap up the user testing session with a group discussion on how the product could be improved. Comparing and discussing their respective user experience helps generate new ideas and consensus on how the product should go forward.

Decision to continue with MVP development

At the end of the data product validation phase, a decision needs to be made about whether the data product qualifies for the development of the MVP. This should consider all aspects from the data product design phase and the data product validation phase. It only makes sense to continue if a data product is feasible and compliant, creates a high enough business impact and is desired by the users. If the decision is negative, it is possible to go back to the initial business problem statement that the data product aimed to solve and to repeat the data product ideation phase to find another, better data product idea that can solve the problem.

CASE STUDY
Data product ideation at a consumer goods company

A possible format for designing and validating products in a short timeframe is design sprints. Here, the whole process of creating product ideas, defining the best solution, validating, prototyping and testing a product is reduced to one week. Design sprints are predominantly about engaging stakeholders and focusing on the user perspective, while deep-dive analyses for the business, technical and compliance perspective are only a minor part of this workshop. There are usually about five to nine participants who consist of representatives of the engineering team, business stakeholders and subject matter experts as well as a moderator who guides the session. Design sprints are most suitable for well-defined tasks, such as adding a number of additional features to an existing product or building a prototype X for department Y to solve problem Z. However, they can also be useful to kick-start an entirely new product, as this case study at a consumer goods company (Buy&Sell) illustrates.

Monday: Ideation and problem statement

On day one, the main aim is to generate ideas and a problem statement that the final data product should solve. Buy&Sell wants to explore solutions to streamline their billing process for their suppliers with the help of a data product. Participants consist of a moderator, a data scientist, two software developers, a product designer, a product owner, a business stakeholder from the purchasing department, a senior stakeholder from the superincumbent supply chain department and two specialists working in the purchasing department. After a short introduction round and a warm-up exercise, the moderator asks the two specialists to describe their work and even demonstrate the current billing process on screen. The other participants ask questions and take how-might-we notes – that is, they formulate their thoughts in the following specific format on sticky notes: 'How might we visualize the project's progress?' or 'How might we allow the machine to make recommendations for the data entry?' These notes should be quite specific and contain some element of design, so that the design focus of the workshop is clear from the start. The how-might-we notes are first collected, then the moderator asks the design sprint team to organize them according to topics. At this point, the subject matter experts leave the workshop, but they remain available for follow-up questions. Now, the participants start to sketch a user journey map together with the moderator. Here, they focus on the most important steps and do not get lost in details. At the end of the day, they agree on the problem statement for this design sprint.

Tuesday: Sketching solutions

On Tuesday, the focus is on researching solutions and on sketching as many solutions as possible to filter out the best one in the end. Since the billing process optimization issue has been discussed in the purchasing department for a while now, the participating purchasing department business stakeholder has already prepared a number of examples from other tools and departments that she presents to the other workshop participants at the beginning of the workshop. The product designer draws the most prominent features of the respective products as examples for the pinboard. Then, the moderator asks the participants to develop and sketch ideas of their own that would solve the stated problem. This should also include ideas out of the box – the aim is to create as many ideas as possible, while validation is part of the next day.

Wednesday: Validation

On this day, the workshop team make a decision on the best solution, which can also be a combination of a number of ideas. First, everyone presents their ideas from the day before. Based on the emerging discussion, a decision on the main direction of the product is made. The moderator plays a major role here by ensuring that discussions remain focused and come to a timely conclusion. It should also be clear beforehand who makes the final decision, for example senior business stakeholders. In our case, the team agree on a solution together. Throughout the second part of the day, a detailed user story mapping based on the winning ideas is worked out as a group exercise.

Thursday: Rapid prototyping

Now it is time to build a prototype based on the detailed user story mapping. While the business stakeholders take a break from the design sprint workshop today, the other participants decide to build their prototype as a clickable wireframe that looks and feels similar to what their envisioned product would be like. The moderator takes care that no new ideas are incorporated into the prototype, but that the team stick to the user story that was agreed upon the day before. By the end of the day, a clickable wireframe is ready to be tested.

Friday: Testing

While preparing the design sprint, the product owner and the business stakeholders chose a suitable group of six users that should test the prototype. Some of the test users, who have different levels of seniority, come from the purchasing department, others come from other departments within the supply chain department. The moderator briefly introduces the purpose of the prototype and the desired outcome of the testing session, which is detailed feedback on content, usability and efficiency. While the users test the prototype, the design sprint team members take notes on their comments and any difficulties that they might encounter when testing the wireframe.

A final discussion round with all the relevant business stakeholders at Buy&Sell and the design sprint team summarizes the main findings on the usefulness of the prototype and opportunities for improvement. If the business stakeholders decide to go forward with the product, this can serve as the basis for a product roadmap.

LESSONS LEARNED AND PITFALLS FOR DATA PRODUCT DESIGN

Focus on the big picture first, details will follow

It is tempting to try to plan everything right from the start – details on UI elements, data structures and algorithms. However, with an agile methodology, this is not necessary and can even be counterproductive. The product will naturally evolve as it obtains continuous feedback via sprint reviews, user testing sessions, machine learning model evaluations and code reviews from data scientists, engineers, users and business stakeholders. Building a data product is truly a team effort on a long-term basis and to keep everyone engaged it is important to value and incorporate their ideas. Product managers should keep an open mind about continuously improving the product while following the problem statement that the product was designed for.

Examine and use what is already available

When generating product ideas and creating product visions, it is easy to be enthusiastic about starting everything from scratch. However, products and artefacts that already exist in the company or even externally should be thoroughly examined first, because this might save months of product development and create synergies. Strategic considerations can play a role here, too. For example, a product manager might reach out to a squad that has already built a well-established platform in the company and offer to add another data product to this platform. This would save the development time for an own platform, generate an integrated product environment and create additional buy-in from other stakeholders within the company.

The success of ideation workshops depends on participants and scope

Participants for the ideation workshops should be chosen to optimally represent the data product domains and different levels of hierarchy. If the domain is sales and marketing, it could include, for example, representatives from product marketing, digital marketing, customer service, brand management and other related areas. Depending on the size of the organization, it can be fruitful to further split up the group into sub-domains for the ideation workshops, to keep the number of people and topics manageable.

Checklist for data product design

This checklist can be used as a template to describe a data product during the data product ideation and design phases.

CHECKLIST

Idea title: Give your data product idea a short title.

Data: Describe what data is needed to implement the data product.

Algorithm: Describe what the algorithm should do.

Action: Describe how the result of the data product should be used to create business value.

Feasibility: How much effort is it to implement the data product?

1 Very low.

2 Low.

3 Medium.

4 High.

5 Very high.

Impact: How much potential business benefit is created by the data product?

1 Very low.

2 Low.

3 Medium.

4 High.

5 Very high.

Product perspective:

- What are the product features?
- Which functionalities should be in the MVP?
- What are the interface design requirements?

Business perspective:

- What is the business impact of the data product?
- Who are the relevant business stakeholders?

User perspective:

- Which users will use the data product?
- What would be desired user journeys?

Feasibility:

- Is enough data available?
- Can systems consume and feed data as required by the data product?

Compliance:

- Are there legal or regulatory showstoppers?
- Would it be ethical to implement the data product?

Summary and conclusion

Data product design follows three phases. First, ideas for new data products need to be generated and filtered. Second, the prioritized data products need to be defined from five perspectives. The product perspective looks at the data product itself: which kinds of product features does the data product need to have to generate value from data, and what could be a feasible roadmap for these product features? The business perspective defines the business impact that is created by the data product on metrics in the product domain, and the key business stakeholders for the data product. The user perspective defines who will be using the data product and their respective needs. The technical perspective looks at the data and the solution architecture needed to deliver the data product, and its feasibility and quality requirements. And finally, the compliance perspective investigates whether there are showstoppers with regard to corporate rules, regulations, legal boundaries and ethical considerations. Third, data products are validated, for example, by applying rapid prototyping. If the user acceptance of a data product is doubtful, user tests with mock-ups and other prototypes can be conducted to verify the user acceptance. As part of the technical feasibility assessment, data needs to be provided and understood, and the quality of the data is tested. The potential business impact of a data product is further examined and evidence for the business impact is collected. The compliance perspective can also be subject to validation and assumptions should be confirmed. Once a data product is successfully validated, it can enter the data product delivery planning phase.

Note

1 European Commission, High-Level Expert Group on Artificial Intelligence, 2019. https://ec.europa.eu/digital-single-market/en/high-level-expert-group-artificial-intelligence (archived at https://perma.cc/HEW3-VFUU)

04

Data product delivery

LEARNING OBJECTIVES FOR THIS CHAPTER

- Learn how to scope and plan the delivery of the MVP of a data product.
- Learn how to develop and deploy a data product following agile principles.
- Learn how to operate a data product in DevOps and MLOps mode.
- Learn how to scale a data product across the organization.
- Learn why data scientists should also be responsible for machine learning during the operation of the models.

Key principles for delivering data products

Only a few successfully validated data products pass the funnel from data product design to data product delivery and make it to a stage in which they are actually implemented. These data products have great business potential and will contribute to the overall strategy and vision, have been evaluated as technically feasible and compliant and are desired by intended users.

Data product delivery is the time when great data product ideas are turned into reality using an agile implementation approach. Machine learning models are now fully implemented, tested and deployed in production.

FIGURE 4.1 The three phases of delivering data products

The delivery of data products follows three phases:

1 **Planning the delivery of data products:** Define the MVP further and plan development, deployment, operation and scaling.

2 **Developing and deploying data products:** Develop and document the data product in agile sprints and deploy it into production.

3 **Operating and scaling data products:** Run, support, expand and maintain the data product and scale it to further business scopes to increase value.

Key principles for planning the delivery of data products

Before the actions happens, a *data product delivery planning phase* is needed. As part of the product design, the set of product features that form the MVP have already been defined, and these need to be further detailed out in the form of requirements. The delivery organization, context and scope, system architecture and interfaces, data and machine learning models, and deployment and operation have to be planned accordingly.

KEY PRINCIPLES
Planning the delivery of data products

• The scope of the MVP needs to be further refined by creating epics, user stories, business and engineering requirements and acceptance criteria.

• The architecture, data model, machine learning model, system interfaces, deployment and operation processes of the data product need to be defined.

- A micro services architecture approach should be applied whenever possible by creating many software components rather than one big monolith.

- The technical environments planned for developing, testing and running the data product should match as much as possible, to remove friction.

- Processes, responsibilities and service level agreements (SLAs) for data product operation need to be established addressing the requirements.

Key principles for developing and deploying data products

The delivery of data products starts during the *data product development and deployment phase*. The data product delivery planning has not created a fixed plan but rather a foundation and framework for agile delivery planning with defined goals, context, organization, budget and time plan for a successful data product delivery. The actual data product development takes place in a series of agile sprints of the data product squad team with regular reviews with the stakeholders. All software code, including code for infrastructure and deployment, has to follow coding, documenting and testing standards to ensure maintainability, scalability, security, reliability, adaptiveness and user acceptance.

KEY PRINCIPLES
Developing and deploying data products

- The MVP is delivered following agile development processes, such as Scrum and Kanban.

- DevOps principles are adhered to, which ensure the smooth integration of development and operations, including the continuous integration and continuous delivery of software code.

- Deployment processes, software tests and infrastructure set-up should be automated as much as possible and version controlled.

- During product delivery, stakeholders and users need to be managed and feedback collected to adapt and revise the data product as early as possible.

- Accompanying the go live of a data product, users might need training, and business processes might need to be adapted.

Key principles for operating and scaling data products

The real work of developing a data product often only begins when it goes live as an MVP. A large list of value-adding functionalities is usually taken out of the scope of the MVP to ensure a fast time to market, and now these need to be gradually implemented. Data products need to be supported and customer and user relationship management is absolutely central. The right level of service and support must be provided, and the feedback of the customers and users must be listened to and acted on. Often, the value of the data product can be multiplied if it is rolled to other markets or parts of the business, and therefore scaling of data products is a key value driver that requires special attention and resource planning. And, finally, at some point most data products reach their end of life and are phased out. There are many aspects that need to be considered when data products enter their operations and scaling phase that will be covered in this section.

KEY PRINCIPLES
Operating and scaling data products

- Infrastructure and software are monitored on an ongoing basis.

- Problems, bugs and user pain points are fixed fast and systematically.

- Operational processes are constantly optimized and further automated.

- Machine learning models and data quality are monitored, and regular machine learning model retraining and updates are scheduled.

- A trust relationship with users should be established through a high product quality, constant user feedback, great user support and by fulfilling SLAs.

- The data product is enhanced with new additional features that have been not in the scope of the MVP but are prioritized among other product features.

- The aim is to roll out data products to other scopes to increase its value fast.

- A data product is retired when it is no longer usable, or when it is replaced.

Planning the delivery of data products

Before the data product delivery can start, lean agile planning is necessary to ensure that the delivery can be effective and efficient once it begins. There are a number of aspects that should be considered as part of the data product delivery planning, including the definition of user stories and acceptance criteria for each product feature. Moreover, the governance, organization and communication approach for the data product delivery need to be defined, ie who makes which type of decision, who has what role during the delivery, and which stakeholders are informed or involved at which stage. Further, the context and scope for the MVP of the data product, in particular the business context, the system context and what is inside or outside the scope need to be further detailed out. If the delivery planning phase has been executed well, development and deployment can usually run quite smoothly as most important architectural and software design decisions have already been made during planning.

Planning the delivery governance, organization, resources and budget

One part of the data product delivery organization is the selection of the data product squad team that will implement the data product led by the responsible data product manager (see also Chapter 5 on capabilities and organization). The other part of the delivery organization that needs to be determined and fixed before the data product delivery starts is the stakeholders who should be included in the sprint planning and prioritization process and in the user acceptance tests of the deliverables. There might also be a steering council and committees that need to be informed about or involved in the data product delivery. Furthermore, a decision can be made on the maximum number of sprint deliveries of the MVP due to resource constraints and budget allocations, which can influence how many functional and non-functional requirements should be included in the MVP, and may result in a reduction in the number of product features to be implemented. This might change the original planned scope of the MVP. As the data product delivery follows agile principles, planning and governance are done in a light way.

Agile planning of data products

Machine learning models that run in production and scale require more and more software engineering and architecture competences. In contrast to traditional development processes, which follow a waterfall approach, not every detail needs to be decided, planned and fixed during the delivery planning phase of a data product. The traditional project management workflow involves the sequential steps of planning the project, delivering milestone 1, milestone 2, etc, until delivering the final product and obtaining feedback. In machine learning and software development, this method has not proven to be successful, since there is always an inherent element of chaos involved irrespective of the quality of the developed machine learning models and the written code that makes the originally planned project steps obsolete and requires a different method of obtaining feedback. The goal of data product delivery planning is, rather, to provide a frame in which agile development processes can operate. It gives guidance, clarity and context and allows those involved to consider and reflect on more critical and challenging aspects of delivery early on. At the same time, we can expect any plan to be at least partially, and sometimes fully, revised as new insights surface during agile delivery that require adjustments to and corrections of the original plan. So we have a plan, but it is not static – it is a living document that changes and adapts during data product delivery.

Many of the unexpected occurrences that can happen on the technical or business side during data product development can be resolved using agile planning.

On the technical side this could be, for example:

- The data model structure or data sources change and require adaptation.
- Issues of disharmony between different elements of a data product, eg that the pipeline that adds new code to the tool does not work because the newly developed testing framework throws error after error due to wrong data formats, or the coordination in the display of a

table in the frontend fails due to the alteration of a specific data type in the backend.

- The technical solution already planned to solve a specific problem does not function as expected, eg the machine model cannot fulfil the quality criteria and requires adaptations.

On the business side this could be, for example:

- The business owners might request a new feature.
- Business metrics change and the target variable of the machine learning model must be altered.
- New regulations may demand major alterations in the current functionality of the data product.

In order to manage this element of chaos and to bridge the gap between business expectations and delivered data products, agile methods are state of the art in both machine learning and software development.

Product requirements and planning perspectives for the delivery of the data product MVP

There are certain expectations that a data product needs to fulfil, which are usually defined in the 'product requirements' document for the MVP. These expectations differ from organization to organization, data product to data product, its users, stakeholders and the technical environments. A number of different aspects can be applied to better plan data product delivery. The context and scope of each data product should be detailed out, there should be quality and testing standards, expectations towards architecture, interfaces and supplied data, and standards for deployment and operations. An example of a requirement as part of a 'product requirements' document could be, for instance: 'The data product needs to connect to all specified systems with a response time of <2 seconds.'

ASPECTS THAT CAN BE ADDRESSED IN THE DEFINITION OF THE 'PRODUCT REQUIREMENTS'

The business and system context

The business context shows the data product in the context of the organization, for example which business processes are affected by the data product and which departments need to be involved in using the data product. The system context shows which other IT applications and systems need to communicate with the data product and require system interfaces. The business and system context can have an implication for the product requirements, eg the data product must work well together with a specific business process.

Software and ML quality, documentation and testing standards

Software code should be tested, documented, integrated and ready for release. The general standards for testing, documentation, integration and release readiness of software code need to be defined in the definition of done. All machine learning models should be also tested and documented, and there might be minimum standards for machine model prediction quality included in the product requirements.

Architecture standards

The entire development should follow micro services architecture standards that prevent the creation of large software code monoliths that can become quickly unmanageable and difficult to maintain. There will be certain expectations with regard to the security, reliability, responsiveness and performance of the solution architecture. The architectural standards for the data product delivery should be therefore part of the definition of done.

Legal and compliance

Legal and compliance issues have been identified during data product design, and some might have implications for the product requirements, eg personal data must be always anonymized before machine learning training and execution.

Data model and data quality

The data models that are delivered by other systems to run the data product need to be documented and minimal requirements with regard to data quantity and quality should be defined as part of the definition of done.

Deployment and operations

Technical standards, processes, responsibilities and SLAs for data product deployment and operation should be outlined in a way that addresses user needs and is feasible.

Creating epics, user stories and acceptance criteria for product features of the MVP

During the data product design phase, the MVP was defined as a set of product features. These are now broken down into epics and user stories, and prioritized as product backlog items (PBIs) in the product backlog. To do that, one or more workshops with the product squad team are organized by the data product manager, including data scientists, data engineers and developers and potentially even some future users of the data product. For each product feature, one epic is defined by the team in the product backlog. Each epic consists of a number of user stories, again included as PBIs in the backlog. A user story is formulated in the following way: 'As a <role> I can <capability>, so that <receive benefit>'. For example, a user story could be: 'As a customer, I want to know when I can expect my delivery, so I can ask my neighbour to accept it for me.' The role could also be an internal customer or a data scientist who needs support from a data engineer. For every user story, further business and engineering requirements can be defined. All user stories taken together form the functional requirements for the product feature epic. The general rule should be that user stories can be completed within one sprint, while epics usually take more than one sprint to complete. Nevertheless, making epics too big should be avoided by splitting them into several smaller epics if necessary. Each epic and user story should have acceptance

criteria that define when they are actually done and which requirements they need to fulfil to be accepted. Finally, all epics and user
stories are put into an order of prioritization by the data product
manager based on the needs of the business sponsors, users and
customers.

Defining non-functional requirements for the MVP

It is very tempting to focus on the functional requirements of the
product, but other requirements regarding performance, reliability, machine learning model quality standards, up-time, compliance,
legal obligations and IT security should be incorporated at an
early stage. Such requirements that relate to how well a data product behaves are often referred to as non-functional requirements.
An example of a non-functional requirement of a data product
could be the response time of the API that is the interface to the
machine learning model, eg the API needs to respond within 1
second, or the prediction quality of the output of the machine
learning model, eg the R2 score of the machine learning model
needs to be constantly above 0.85 and should be calculated and
tested on a weekly basis. Such non-functional requirements should
be defined jointly by the product squad team (again, including
data scientists, data engineers, developers and facilitated by the
data product manager). There are three ways of defining the non-
functional requirements. The first way is to create a new user story
for the non-functional requirement and include it as a new item in
the product backlog, eg 'As a user, I expect the API of the data

FIGURE 4.2 How to create functional requirements for a data product

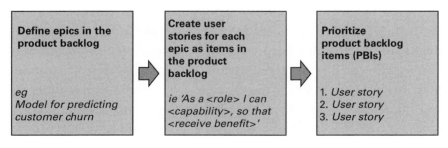

FIGURE 4.3   How to define non-functional requirements for the data product

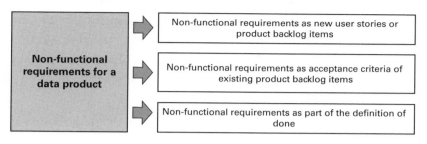

product to respond within 1 second, so I can integrate the results in near real-time into my website and satisfy my website visitors.' The second way is to integrate a non-functional requirement into an existing user story as an acceptance criteria for the PBI, eg 'As a customer, I want to know when I can expect my delivery, so I can ask my neighbour to accept it for me' gets the acceptance criteria that 'The machine learning model needs to have a R2 score of above 0.85.' The third way is to also include non-functional requirements into the definition of the 'product requirements' when they are relevant for all product features, eg 'All content must be in English and French.'

Planning the roadmap for the data product

The information obtained throughout the product design and validation phase and the product features in and out of scope of the MVP should be used to create the product roadmap. The product roadmap serves as the main point of orientation for everyone involved in the product design and delivery process. If anything goes in a different direction than planned, it can be quickly identified here. Desired features for the MVP as well as the timeline and fixed dates for user testing sessions and release dates should be included in the product roadmap. Efforts on the business side, such as preparations for compliance topics or dates for leadership validation, could be incorporated as well if they have been identified as potential implementation risks.

Kick-off workshop before sprint with the squad team and stakeholders

Finally, the data product delivery starts with a kick-off planning workshop with the entire data product squad team and the internal stakeholders, to review whether everything is in place to trigger the data product development.

Developing and deploying data products

The *data product development and deployment phase* is often considered the exciting part of the data product delivery process, as most of the software and machine model implementation work is done during this phase. This involves the creation of a production-ready machine learning model, which usually requires refactoring, refining and hardening of the machine learning model from the data product validation phase. Moreover, backend and frontend functionalities, system interfaces, deployment pipelines and automated test scripts need to be developed as defined by the scope of the MVP. Most software tests and deployment actions should be automated as part of the software development. The result is the go live of the MVP of a data product that is maintainable, scalable, secure, reliable, flexible and accepted by the users. Often, changes in business processes and training of users are required and these should be in line with the change strategy.

Productizing and automating machine learning models

There is a great difference between a machine learning prototype and a productive machine learning model. During the data product validation phase, the machine learning model prototype is created, usually based on data from CSV files extracted from the supplying systems that are manually cleansed and prepared to generate the features and the target variable necessary for model training and testing. During the data product development phase, it is time to automate all processes to get data from the source systems, to clean and prepare the data, to generate features and target variables and apply and refresh the machine learning models. Moreover, the machine models often need to be refactored, further stabilized and tested to achieve robustness during operations. Note that in some cases the data loading, preparation and running of the machine learning might be not fully automated, to faster develop the MVP.

CHECKLIST

What is needed to turn a machine learning prototype to a machine learning product:

- fine-tuning the machine learning model to increase the prediction quality;
- refactoring the machine learning model code to make it easier to maintain;
- testing the machine learning model with synthetic data that simulates unusual situations;
- creating automated data pipelines that extract, transform and load data and create features and output variables;
- setting up automated data loads;
- continuous testing and monitoring of the machine learning model.

Data products do not come as pure machine learning algorithms – they need to be supplied with database connections and data transformations and are usually supplemented with complex backend and frontend software functionalities. Developing and deploying data products therefore draws heavily on methods and methodologies from modern software development and should be regarded as agile software development projects.

Agile methods for data product development

The entire data product, including the improvement and hardening of machine learning models, can be managed within the same agile frameworks that are used in software development. In essence, agile software development entails the incremental delivery of a product with regular feedback from the customer or business owner. It is based on four values and 12 principles that form the Agile Manifesto, which was published in 2001 by a group of software developers.[1] The Agile Manifesto advocates close collaboration within the developer team and with the business owner and calls for flexibility from both parties. A variety of methodologies have developed that fulfil the Agile Manifesto's requirements and the two most common ones will be explored below, ie Scrum and Kanban. There is no right or wrong with regard to when to apply which method as this depends on the context and culture. Some developer teams even use a combination or mix of both methods to make them fit to their environment (known as 'Scrumban').

SCRUM
Scrum is the most popular framework for agile development. It has strictly defined roles and processes that partly resemble traditional project management.

The scrum master keeps the overview and ensures that the Scrum process is adhered to. The product owner is responsible for the product backlog and prioritizes the work. The development team works on the product backlog items until they fulfil the definition of done.

The following events serve as integral parts of the Scrum framework:

- sprint planning;
- daily stand-up;
- backlog refinement;
- sprint review;
- sprint retrospective.

A sprint is a fixed time interval or increment during which a specific amount of work is planned and conducted. It usually lasts between two and four weeks. During the sprint planning, the product owner presents new product backlog items that the team should work on in the upcoming sprint. The product backlog items are discussed and the work effort is estimated. Daily stand-ups function as briefs that help identify any issues encountered by some team members that other team members may be able to help out with. Backlog refinements are meetings that give the team members the opportunity to ask the product owner if anything is unclear with the product backlog items. They also give the product owner the opportunity to re-prioritize some product backlog items and clean up the product backlog. The sprint reviews serve as points of interaction with the development team and the stakeholders to show the progress that has been made in the past sprint, that is the past increment, and to obtain feedback, which in turn can be used as input for the next product backlog items in the upcoming sprint planning. Finally, in the sprint retrospective, which takes place after the sprint review, the development team reflects on the past sprint, and which aspects of their work together can be kept and which should be changed in order to perform better in the next sprint.

KANBAN

In comparison to Scrum, Kanban provides fewer fixed roles and events. Everything is centred around the Kanban board, which inverts the Scrum product backlog list to a board with several columns that each have distinct functions. Instead of planning in detail who is going to work on which specific task in the upcoming sprint, the development team members select product backlog items that are in the 'ready' column, and shift them to the 'in progress' column and finally to the 'review' column once they are done. The product owner presents the product backlog items during the queue replenishment meetings and discusses with the team members what should be done. After the stakeholders have reviewed the progress, the product backlog items from the 'review' column are shifted to the 'done' column. Aspects of Scrum are often incorporated into Kanban, for example regular sprint review meetings are held to obtain feedback from the stakeholders. Which method is more suitable for a development team really depends on the team's preferences. Scrum in general provides the timeboxing advantage and offers a clear structure and planning certainty. Teams that are just starting out with agile methods may prefer the rigid structure and clearly defined roles of Scrum. Working with Kanban can be more efficient, though, since fewer meetings are needed. With the Kanban board as the central switch point to monitor the team's progress, it can be easier to recognize bottlenecks early and fit the different columns to the specific team's needs.

However, irrespective of which agile framework a team chooses, an important point to note is that in agile settings, teams are basically self-organizing, even though there might be specific roles such as scrum master or product owner. Requests for the product are coming in from outside and need to be dealt with, yet they need to be dealt with according to the team's decisions. Every team member should take equal responsibility for the product development and play an active role in constantly improving collaboration.

Coding and documentation standards for data product development

Both data scientists and data engineers can be considered developers as soon as they write software code (which they should do, at the latest during the data product development phase). As many data scientists do not come from a software engineering background, it is particularly important to establish clear rules and standards for coding, documentation and testing during data product development. Apart from basic rules for coding, such as writing clean code that serves a single purpose with one function and is well documented, communication among developers is key to success. Any interaction among developers that involves explaining code to each other helps find the best solution under the respective circumstances, and supports everyone to become better at what they do and learn from each other.

IMPROVING COMMUNICATION BETWEEN DEVELOPERS

Many approaches can help improve communication between developers and the level of software code quality. Here are some examples:

- **Pair programming:** Two developers work together at one workstation, with one writing the code while the other observes and reviews it.

- **Mob programming:** The same as pair programming, except the whole team works jointly at one workstation to solve problems together.

- **Hackathons:** A team of developers and product managers works together on a collaborative project in a very limited amount of time to create a prototype.
- **Code reviews:** The developer walks through the code with another developer who has not been involved in programming the code to find improvements.
- **Model reviews:** The data scientist walks through the machine learning model, the set of features and the target variable with another data scientist to identify potential modelling issues and statistical irregularities.
- **Data pipeline reviews:** The data engineer walks through the data loading and transformation steps with another data engineer and/or data scientist to identify potential data processing problems when calculating the features and target variables.
- **Rubber duck review:** The developer explains the software code regularly to a rubber duck. This can in fact increase the developer's level of code quality.

You should aim to establish a culture of communication in your developer team. In DevOps, this culture of communication is crucial, because every line of code has to be reviewed by another developer before it is merged into the main branch. The reviewing developer may question some of the decisions that the other developer has made, which ultimately allows them to discover bugs or inefficiencies and improve the code. This process also makes it possible to distribute responsibilities throughout the team, so that everyone feels more responsible for the whole product.

Testing standards for data product development

One of the most effective methods for ensuring machine learning model and software code quality of a data product is rigorous testing. Each data product development should contain a testing concept, from a very basic level to the overall product. Quality tests based on the standard statistics and other validation methods are used for machine learning models by splitting the production data into training and testing data, and should be selected to best fit the type of machine learning model and the type of problem. Moreover, machine learning models are typically implemented in a programming language, usually Python, relying on a number of open source packages (eg Pandas, NumPy, SciPy) and need, on top of the machine learning prediction quality measures, the same level of testing as any other normal software code. The most basic level of software code tests are unit tests, which simply test whether a function works as intended. The next level of software code tests are component and integration tests, which test whether the different components of a product work together as intended even after a new feature or function has been added or changed. These integration tests should be integrated as automatic tests into the product pipeline, so that new commits can only be added to the product code base if they have passed the tests. Manual tests should regularly be conducted as well, either by the developer or by the data product manager, to ensure that the product still fully functions and displays the envisaged UI. Finally, load tests assess whether a large number of users can safely use the product without experiencing any performance problems. As part of the compliance process, you may also want to incorporate penetration tests well before the release date, to ensure that all the necessary IT security measures are in place.

Continuous integration and continuous delivery of data products

Right at the beginning of the data product development process, you should set up the most important environments for the data product, ie the development, test, stage and production environments. The continuous integration/continuous delivery (CI/CD) pipeline consists of a number of jobs and stages, including automated tests, that should be configured by an experienced data engineer. Only if all jobs have been successfully passed will the code be incorporated into the main branch and into the respective environment. Each developer will have their local environment where they write their code. This is also the first environment in which they test the new code. In fact, one of the top five of the most frequently uttered phrases in developer teams is likely to be: 'But this works on my machine!' However, the new code also has to work in combination with everybody else's committed code. In the development environment you can test whether this is really the case, because here everyone's contributions are combined and you might find that there are conflicts among newly committed pieces of code that need to be resolved before they can be merged into the development environment.

CHECKLIST

- **Continuous integration** essentially means to integrate new code into the software product on a frequent basis, ie developers should merge their respective feature branch in which they have been committing new code into the main branch as often as possible.
- **Continuous delivery and deployment** means updating the stage and production environments as frequently as possible. In order to reach these goals, a CI/CD pipeline needs to be set up that runs automatically after each commitment of code and after each merging of branches, including deploying to different environments. The CI/CD pipeline ideally includes a number of rigorous testing procedures, thereby ensuring that only code that passes these tests can be deployed in the respective environment.

The test environment serves its purpose by testing new code, and is sometimes left out, while the stage environment closely resembles the production environment and therefore enables new code to be tested under conditions that mimic the production environment. It can be used for demos and presentations for the stakeholders, and it can be used to determine if the product is still fully functioning after code changes have been committed. This is a crucial step before deployment to the production environment, since this is the actual environment that the customer accesses when using the product. Any change during operations mode should be thoroughly tested in the stage environment before deploying it to the production environment.

Stakeholder and go live management

Stakeholders can be involved in a data product in different ways, ie as investors, users, compliance agents or business domain experts. Stakeholders have a specific interest that drives them to care and chaperone the product, which makes them key assets that need to be cherished and closely involved in the data product delivery process. To make matters more complicated, stakeholders more often than not come from a business perspective with little or no experience in data and AI topics. It is the data product manager's responsibility to bridge the gap between the stakeholders' business and/or domain perspective and the product team's agile and technical point of view. This means that every point of interaction should be carefully managed. Working with stakeholders entails boiling complex technical issues down to their business-related essence. In turn, it also means translating the stakeholder's requests or feedback into clear-cut advice for the product delivery team.

GROUND RULES

The following ground rules can help data product managers build a good relationship with stakeholders during the product delivery process:

- **Deliver on your promises:** Deliver good quality at decent cost on time.

- **Be transparent:** If a problem emerges, inform them immediately while offering solutions.

- **Set up regular meetings** to report on progress (eg jour fixes or sprint reviews), not only by passively presenting the product, but also by giving them an early opportunity to test the product themselves (eg via user testing).

- **Manage expectations:** Be clear on what the product features do and do not entail, and which trade-offs exist among them (ie in terms of model performance and model metrics).

- **Integrate their business domain knowledge into the data product:** Stakeholders are often domain experts and should be actively consulted by building their business logic into the data product, eg via business rules or by defining which model performance metrics to aim for (eg minimizing false positives vs minimizing false negatives, see Chapter 6 for details).

- **Be flexible:** Incorporate changes or new features as the stakeholders demand, while being clear what this means for the project's budget and delivery time.

- **However, you should be able to say no:** If a feature request by the stakeholder is not backed up by user research or puts the product at risk in any way, it is the data product manager's duty to deny the feature request if necessary. Clearly communicating the reasons for doing so and closely involving the stakeholders in discussions related to product strategy allows a healthy relationship to be maintained even if there are divergent points of view.

- **Build a relationship:** Not only between yourself as the data product manager and the stakeholders, but also between the stakeholders and the product delivery team by scheduling meetings that require the participation of both sides, for example at a kick-off meeting or MVP workshop.

As part of the go live of a data product, it is important to make sure that users have sufficient information on how to use the data product properly via demo videos, help pages, tooltips or a live tutorial from the data product manager or an experienced user. The go live of a data product often occurs alongside significant business process changes that need to be communicated and might require the provision of training and change management for users and business stakeholders. In addition, before the data product is launched, data product managers should set the scene for the users in order to manage expectations and to obtain valuable feedback. It is the task of data product managers to inform users and stakeholders that this data product is an MVP and highly depends on their feedback in order to improve it further during data product operations and scaling.

Operating and scaling data products

Many business stakeholders do not realize that a large proportion of the work needed for a data product actually starts after the go live of the data product during the *data product operating and scaling phase*. A data product is brought live as MVP and therefore includes only the most essential functionalities. After going live, there are typically many bug fixes and minor improvements to be done. Sprint after sprint, new functionalities and product features might be prioritized by the data product manager and are added to the data product by applying continuous delivery and integration. Each data product, including the underlying machine learning models and infrastructure, needs to be closely monitored, supported and enhanced. Machine learning models need to be retrained with new data and, if the data has changed its structure, machine learning models need to be revised. Successful data products can often be applied in further parts of the business, eg in a different market, production plant or business division, to increase the business value. Finally, a decision needs to be made when a data product should not be used anymore and taken out of operation and support.

From DevOps to MLOps: Applying the principles of DevOps to data and AI

While agile methods enable the members of the developer team to effectively work together, they do not incorporate data product operation. DevOps is a philosophy that aims to dissolve the inherent conflict between developing a product and thereby adding new code versus actually deploying the product and aiming to serve a business purpose with it. Adding new code may disturb the smooth functioning of the product; it is therefore very important to establish mechanisms to minimize risks and ensure a stable product. DevOps serves this purpose by actively intertwining development and operations, so that their classic separation is a mere silo mentality of the past. Following the DevOps principles first and foremost means to think of the operation phase from day one of product development. This mindset ensures that everyone has the overriding objective in mind: to deliver a functioning data product that the user can work with. DevOps for data and AI, which is referred to as MLOps (a compound of 'machine learning' and 'operations'), has the consequence that data scientists and data engineers are also responsible for the machine learning models and data pipelines during data product operations. Data scientists and data engineers should consider how best to operate and maintain a machine learning model during data product delivery planning and development.

Running and monitoring data products as key activities of MLOps

During the *data product operation phase*, the machine learning model needs to be supplied regularly, or even constantly, with fresh data, which is like oxygen for a data product. The data pipelines are like arteries that transport oxygen, and these need to be monitored and quality controlled 24/7 by building software scripts for data quality profiling with business rules and anomaly detection. The monitoring should provide warnings if data is not loaded correctly, data formats do not match the expectations or the content of data appears to be unusual (eg outliers that are three standard deviations away from the mean in the case of numerical values or unexpected values in the case of non-numeric data fields). Machine learning models need to be retrained with new data regularly to ensure that they capture systematic changes and incorporate new features or business logic adaptations (such as the increase in electric vehicles in the automotive sector). Monitoring also needs to be applied to the entire software code and infrastructure, to ensure smooth operation and fast mitigation of problems.

CHECKLIST

The following aspects need to be monitored during data product operations:

- data loads and data pipelines;
- input data quality;
- backend and frontend software functionalities;
- infrastructure;
- machine learning algorithms and outputs;
- machine learning retraining processes.

Besides ensuring that machine learning models and data pipelines work correctly, there are more aspects that are key to drive customer satisfaction: establishing a strong relationship with customers, providing great customer support, listening to customer feedback and continuously improving the data product once it is in production.

Building great customer support for data products

Establishing a strong relationship with your users consists of three main pillars. First, a decent product quality satisfies the user's needs and avoids any points of frustration. Second, a good customer support system should be in place that quickly reacts to any questions and fixes bugs. Third, a customer feedback system collects valuable information on how to improve the product further. A key element is to set up a robust customer support system, which can react quickly to a variety of different requests. Tier 1 level support consists of a generalist who can answer basic questions on the product functionality and who can make a judgement call on whether the problem presented by the user is a serious bug that should be reported to the next level of support. Tier 2 level support deals with more technical questions and bugs and can provide a higher level of detail, which often requires a data scientist or data engineer with substantial know-how about the data and the machine learning model. If this is not sufficient to help with the customer issue at hand, tier 3 level support should step in. These data specialists have a deep understanding of the data product, ideally because they have developed the machine learning models and programmed the surrounding software themselves, and they can solve problems with the highest level of complexity. Different channels for customer support should be considered, including live chats, telephone and email. The aim is to get back to customers in a short timeframe. Accordingly, the time to resolve an issue should be treated as a key performance indicator (KPI) to improve customer satisfaction with the data product. If the data product is business critical with time-sensitive usage in the company, you may want to think about establishing 24-hour-support, at least for tier 1.

Listening to customer and user feedback to enhance data products

Once the data product is launched, you will receive feedback from users. This can be either via customer support, because bugs are reported and need to be fixed in order to ensure full functionality, or via other channels. Sometimes users report ideas for improvement via customer support as well. It is useful to establish a fixed option for feedback, such as feedback forms, but also a flexible form via customer support, forums and contact forms on the product website, and even direct interaction with a number of users by directly discussing the product and their user experience with them. A third option consists of more analytical approaches, such as A/B testing and site analytics. A/B testing essentially means to release two different versions of a product and testing a hypothesis on the usability of a new version by showing the new and old versions to different subsets of the users. Feedback from both user groups are analysed and compared and the hypothesis is either confirmed or discarded. Site analytics enables a user's behaviour while interacting with the site to be tracked. It can be used to determine whether a specific feature of a product is highly attractive, or not relevant at all. Important metrics include time spent on a site, preferred devices to access the site, and bounce rate.

Implementing improvements and adding new product features

Updates and upgrades to incorporate user feedback improvements and additional data product features are delivered using continuous delivery and integration. Problems and bugs should be thoroughly investigated to find systematic errors and implement sustainable solutions to increase the quality of the data product and improve its maintainability, scalability, security, reliability, adaptiveness and user acceptance. As mentioned above, the DevOps and CI/CD methodologies refer to continuous improvement and the concurrency and coexistence of development and operations. It is therefore of crucial importance to venerate the 80/20 rule, ie the preference to deliver something that is not perfect, but good enough to fulfil the user's needs. Then, the user will provide feedback on how to improve the product further, which in turn can be delivered in an ongoing manner. There are different strategies on how to deploy changes and update the production environment while minimizing the risk of product failure. One example is the blue green deployment. Here, changes are deployed to the production environment, but to the new version of the production environment only. While the DevOps team can test the updated product, the customers still use the previous version. Only if the tests have been successful will customer traffic be allowed on the new version. Similar strategies include partial transfer of customer traffic to the new version while it is being tested.

Scaling and rolling out data products

Data products can often be scaled and rolled out to other business scopes to increase business value, which is done in the *data product scaling phase*. This would include the adaptation of data products to other parts of the business and expanding the functionality of data products to solve more business problems in the same business domain. Therefore, depending on the particular data product, the task is to identify potential ways to scale the data product and to prioritize among them with regard to the value, feasibility and synergy potentials. Scaling a data product to a new scope usually requires an adaptation of the data product to the new scope. For example, data models and the business logic might be different in another production plant or market, and hence the model features, machine learning models and data pre-processing pipelines have to be changed accordingly to make the data product usable in the new scope. In many cases, there are substantial synergies when scaling data products and, therefore, value can be generated faster, eg when features and target variables for machine learning models are the same.

ILLUSTRATIVE EXAMPLES OF SCALING AND ROLLING OUT DATA PRODUCTS

- A machine learning algorithm to predict and prevent customer churn with contract customers in a telecoms company can be adapted and rolled out to prepaid customers and other product lines.

- A machine learning algorithm that interprets sensor signals in a production facility to schedule maintenance activities and prevent breakdowns can be scaled to other production sites and machine types.

- A machine learning algorithm to optimize marketing campaigns in a retail company can be scaled from one geography to others (eg from France to all countries in the European Union).

To scale data products to the new scope identified, data products need to be re-designed to fit the new scopes and adapted, thus they are re-entering the data product design phase for the new scope. This time, it can make even more sense to create standard interfaces and other forms of standardization to realize as many synergies as possible. The data product definition and validation runs a multiple thereof faster than before. Afterwards, the software delivery process runs at an accelerated pace to customize the data product for the new scope. To adapt machine learning models, it makes sense to involve the data scientists who originally created the machine learning model. Rollout managers can be hired to increase the implementation speed and support change management during the data product scaling phase.

Retiring data products

After a few years of successfully operating a data product, there will be a time when it reaches the end of its life, the *data product retirement phase*. This is usually when the data product is to be replaced by a new solution and technology, or when it is no longer needed due to changes in the business. As there might be many interdependencies with the data product that have built up over time, it is important to have a clear plan and roadmap for phasing out the data product at its end of life.

THINGS TO CONSIDER AT THE END OF LIFE OF A DATA PRODUCT

- Have all users been informed about the shutdown of the data product and potentially the replacement solution?

- Have the owners of systems with interfaces to the data product been informed about the end of life of the data product?

- Is the replacement solution in place in time to ensure business continuity?

- Are there any further dependencies on the data product that need to be mitigated?

- Has the data infrastructure been made available to other data products after retiring and existing processes around the data product are finished?

Conduct a post-mortem analysis

Once the data product has reached the end of its lifecycle, the data product development team should take a step back and reflect on the experiences that they gained with that particular data product. The format could be an interactive workshop to discuss what was learned during each step of the product development. This should contain the good, the bad and the ugly, but in a constructive way. This helps the team to improve their processes and incorporate new methods when they deliver the next data product.

CASE STUDY
Data product delivery at a traditional insurance company

A traditional insurance company with a longstanding history in the insurance business offers a wide range of insurance products ranging from automotive insurance, property insurance, travel insurance, health insurance and legal insurance to life insurance and some other niche insurance products. Due to the ageing customer base, the company decides to invest into digital channels and offerings to attract younger customers and cross-sell insurance products to them. The newly established data innovation team call themselves 'the Smart Offers Squad', since this is the first topic that user research has revealed would provide business value for the company. They want to focus on personalized insurance offers to make relevant offers to visitors on the website and give recommendations about other insurance products that might be of interest. The Smart Offers Squad consists of four data scientists, four data engineers, two software developers and two data product managers.

After an ideation workshop with the whole Smart Offers Squad that gave every team member the task of working on a separate idea for a proof of concept, Joanna, the lead data scientist in the Smart Offers Squad, develops a machine learning model on her Jupyter Notebook. Her proof of concept is a recommendation engine that uses the customer profile, existing and past policies of the customers, and recent customer online and offline behaviours as model features to predict which new insurance policy would be the most relevant one. The target variable of the machine learning model is which next insurance product is bought by the customer.

Joanna and her Smart Offers Squad meet up with the company's UX designer to brainstorm how the prototype could be incorporated into the existing customer online portal. Together, they create a number of mock-ups for the widget and test it with customers. They receive positive feedback from the customers and create a product requirements document that contains the functional and non-functional requirements of the recommendation engine product. Now, after successful data product validation of an intelligent recommendation engine, the Smart Offers Squad begin to plan the delivery of the MVP. They develop the product vision that the smart offer is a new web widget within the customer online portal.

In the data product delivery planning phase, Michael, the data product manager of the Smart Offers Squad, meets with the main stakeholders to refine the product vision together. The main stakeholders involved include the tech team lead of the website team and senior representatives from each of the affected data product areas, including automotive insurance, property insurance, travel insurance, health insurance, legal insurance and life insurance. The functional and non-functional product requirements are further refined throughout these meetings, such as the architecture, legal and compliance standards which need to be followed for all data products. Everybody agrees on the features that the MVP should contain and on the design of the UI, with the help of the existing mock-up that is refined as a result of these meetings. Finally, a kick-off meeting with the main stakeholders and the Smart Offers Squad is conducted in which the participants refine the user story mapping, agree on a product roadmap and on their work mode for the development of the data product. For example, they define that they will have an agile development cycle with two-week sprints, including a sprint review with all the main stakeholders after the end of each two weeks.

In order to start the data product development phase, the Smart Offers Squad team meets for the first biweekly sprint planning. Before the first sprint planning meeting, Michael rewrites some of the user stories from the user story mapping meeting as product backlog items, since some of the user stories would require too much development effort to be finished in one sprint. In the first two sprints, the software developer and the data engineers establish the development, testing and staging environment and the CI/CD pipeline. Early in the product development phase, the real data connection to the source systems of the product areas and the web database and the interface to the web application are developed. Now, Joanna refines her original machine learning model in order to incorporate the new data sources, business rules and target metrics that have been agreed on in the product requirements document. She regularly meets up with the domain experts who answer her questions about insurance products and the underlying business logic that are incorporated into the machine learning model.

Throughout the development of the recommendation product, the team regularly deploy their product from the development environment to the testing and staging environments to show the product to their stakeholders during the sprint reviews, but also for testing purposes of their own. Finally, the UI designer creates some detailed designs for the display of the recommendations on the website for each product area. The representatives from the product areas are happy with the design ideas, so the frontend software developer of the team implements the extension of the website user interface accordingly. Throughout the development of the recommendation product, the Smart Offers Squad conducts regular pair programming sessions and model reviews in order to ensure the high quality of their product.

Before the go live of the data product, Michael conducts a workshop with all insurance product teams and the website team to show the completed MVP and start a two-week test period on the test environment. After fixing the last user issues and smaller bugs, the data product is deployed into the production environment using the CI/CD pipelines. The website team integrate the recommendation engine widget into the website in their next sprint. Directly after the go live on the website, the first customers start to use the recommendation widget to obtain information about insurance products that fit their requirements profile. Every week, web analytics data is analysed by the data scientists to understand how the customers are using the information and if they are buying the suggested insurance products. After a few weeks, the machine learning model is retrained to better capture the insurance products that are of greatest interest to the customers. The website team also notices that a few of the suggestions do not make much sense for particular customers. They open up a support ticket with the Smart Offers Squad and immediately Joanna starts to crunch the data with her team to identify the root causes. They find out that there are a number of data quality anomalies in the supplied data from two of the insurance product teams. After a meeting with an insurance domain expert, a solution is found to monitor the data quality with a new automated business rule that is implemented into the monitoring of the data product.

Since a high percentage of customers start to convert and buy the recommended complementary insurance products, the business stakeholders decide that the data product is a success and suggest it should also be used by the call-centre agents. Michael and the Smart Offers Squad team are very excited about this news and create the data product definition of the expanded recommendation engine data product right away. Mock-ups are created that present how the recommendations appear on the screen of the call-centre agents and these are user tested with them. Most of the work is in the integration of the product into the call-centre software, which can be done in several sprints by the squad team, but also requires the support of an external provider to include a number of changes into the next major release of the call-centre software. Moreover, call-centre agents have to be trained to use the new product feature, which is done in three-hour intense training sessions. The recommendation engine is scaled to the new scope and allows call-centre agents to make next best offers to the customers.

Lessons learned and pitfalls for data product delivery

Ways of minimizing the efforts to deliver the MVP faster

It is easy to fall into the trap of over-engineering the MVP. There is a natural tendency to overshoot in making a data product as user-friendly as possible, aiming for technical perfection and designing machine learning algorithms that never make mistakes. Remember that the aim of MVPs is to test the viability of a data product as fast as possible in a real-world environment. This could even mean that a data product goes live with manual data extracts and uploads instead of a systems interface that provides the raw data for the machine learning models. Certain functional and non-functional requirements will need to be fulfilled, otherwise users will not accept the data product or compliance officers might not allow the go live of the data products. Everything else should be reduced to a minimum. After go live, there is plenty of time to add further product features, make the machine learning model even more robust and improve data loading times.

Plan early for deployment, testing and operation

When the MVP date of the data product is approaching rapidly, deployment, testing and operation strategy and implementation should be incorporated early into the product roadmap. This also allows the DevOps approach to be ingrained into the data product development. If every team member has internalized the workflow from the local to the following environments during the early product development stages, it will be easier to follow the procedure during the more hectic days shortly before the MVP launch or the operation phase of the data product. In addition, the testing concept should be set out from the start to implement quality assurance at the very heart of the data product. For the operation phase, the data product manager should plan well ahead before the MVP launch that some basic check marks can be set, including the existence of a backup functionality, the tested process on the integration of updates and bug fixes into the production environment and a set timeline for a beta-release that can be rigorously tested by users from members of the target user group before the MVP goes live.

You built it, you run it, you fix it

Until recently, many data scientists have been hired into teams that were set up as innovation or data labs and tasked with delivering prototypes for great data products. As a consequence, sometimes the data scientists do not take responsibility for the rest of the lifecycle of the data product after validation, which results in in well-designed machine learning models packed in poorly structured software code (or, even worse, written in script languages like R, which makes the deployment of machine learning models much more difficult) being handed over, with the expectation that other technical teams refactor and fix the code, bring it into production and support it. After the go live of the data product, data scientists have often not felt responsible for supporting users of their machine learning models and maintaining and retraining their machine learning models. This is unacceptable. Both data scientists and data engineers should be made responsible for the data product during delivery, deployment and for running the data product after go live, for example, by taking over the second or third level support of the data product and being charged with the retraining of their machine learning models.

Checklist for data product delivery

The following checklist can be used for quality gates between each phase of the data product delivery.

CHECKLIST

Planning:

- The delivery governance, organization, resources and budget are established.
- Functional requirements defined in the form of product backlog items that are in scope of the MVP.
- Software, data and ML quality, documentation and testing standards defined in product requirements.
- Architecture, compliance, deployment and operations standards defined in product requirements.
- Non-functional requirements defined for the MVP.
- Kick-off workshop took place before development.

Development and deployment:

- Squad teams work in agile sprints.
- Machine learning model fine-tuned and refactored.
- Data infrastructure set up and deployable.
- Automated data preparation pipelines and data loads established and tested with machine learning model.
- User and/or machine learning interfaces and other backend functionalities developed and tested.
- All code documented, tested and release ready.
- Users are fully onboarded and ready for go live.
- Data product automatically deployed and live.

Operation:

- Implement DevOps principles, including continuous integration and continuous delivery.
- Apply constant monitoring of all aspects of the data product, including the smooth running of the software functionalities, infrastructure and the data pipelines.
- Retrain the model continuously with newly available data and monitor the results.

- Establish a high-quality customer support system with tier 1, tier 2 and tier 3 level support appropriate for the requirements and business criticality of the data product.
- Collect customer feedback and use it to improve the data product further.
- Decide on a deployment strategy to upgrade the product during the operation phase.

Scaling:

- Where possible, apply standardization such as standard interfaces to facilitate scaling from the start.
- Identify potentials to scale a data product by adapting it to a new scope.
- Adapt the model features, machine learning models and data pre-processing pipelines according to the new scope.
- Involve the data scientists that created the machine learning model for the original data product.
- Hire rollout managers to accelerate implementation.

Retiring:

- Apply a clear roadmap for retiring the data product that includes informing the users and analysing all the existing interdependencies.
- Ensure that the replacement solution is in place.
- Make the existing data infrastructure available for other data products.
- Conduct a post-mortem analysis.

Summary and conclusion

Delivery planning serves as the foundation for the development of the product and provides the set-up for data product delivery. As part of the planning, product features for the MVP are refined on an epic and user story level. The MVP, which is delivered in a number of sprints, usually includes a production-ready machine learning model and the development of the required backend and frontend functionalities, system interfaces, deployment pipelines and automated test scripts that are in scope. Operational processes to monitor, support and maintain the data product should be constantly improved to increase the level of automation and decrease the amount of work that needs to be done. Successful data products might potentially be rolled out to further business scope and retired when they are no longer needed.

Note

1 The Agile Manifesto, Principles behind the Agile Manifesto, 2001. http:// agilemanifesto.org/principles.html (archived at https://perma.cc/L72E-S4WM)

05

Capabilities and agile organization

LEARNING OBJECTIVES FOR THIS CHAPTER
- Learn which capabilities are necessary for data and AI.
- Learn how capabilities can be translated into roles.
- Learn about important design principles for setting up the agile organization.
- Learn about processes and steering logic for data and AI.
- Learn how to build strong and autonomous agile product teams.

Key principles for capabilities and agile organization

A central decision in every data and AI transformation is which capabilities need to be built and how the organization should be established. In Chapter 2, insights were shared on how to design a capability strategy. In this chapter, there will be a deep dive into a number of core capabilities and related roles, responsibilities, organizational set-ups and processes. Roles and responsibilities are defined to build skills and competencies, while the organizational structure focuses on the collaboration and where to place the roles. Processes determine how capabilities interplay and are steered. Technology and governance are also important aspects of building capabilities; these are covered in the next chapter. A lack of alignment sometimes results in building up capabilities and technologies that are not useful to the business and that do not effectively support the data product strategy. Data and AI strategies and initiatives that are led by a purely tech-focused part of an organization often fall into this trap. Likewise, projects run by external consultancies for large corporates have a tendency to go in this direction, as there is an incentive for the consultancy to sign big deals and build technical platforms for a long time before having to show any business benefits.

New core capabilities need to be established to be able to drive the digital transformation through data and AI. In its centre, the data and AI organization has to be built with new roles, responsibilities, organizational structures and processes.

FIGURE 5.1 The four phases of establishing capabilities and agile organization

Capabilities and agile organization can be approached in four phases:

1 **Determining core capabilities for data and AI:** What are the essential things that we need to do to be able to deliver data products and drive the digital transformation through data and AI?

2 **Defining roles and responsibilities:** Which roles are needed to build the capabilities? What should be their responsibilities?

3 **Setting up the agile organization:** How can different roles work together in an organizational structure that supports agility? How should the collaboration between the different roles be organized?

4 **Implementing and adapting processes:** Which core processes need to be implemented for data and AI? Which supporting processes need to be adapted to make digital transformation through data and AI work?

Key principles for determining core capabilities for data and AI

The capability portfolio that is derived from the product portfolio requirements as part of the data and AI strategy outlined in Chapter 2 determines the capability areas that need to be developed. As highlighted before, there are certain core capabilities in data and AI that are usually needed, but which can be adapted depending on the actual capability needs based on the data product strategy.

KEY PRINCIPLES
Determining core capabilities for data and AI

- Core capabilities need to be determined based on the requirements set by the data product strategy.
- A number of core capability areas are needed for most transformations.
- Each capability should support at least one data product domain.
- A capability can require organizational and technological changes.
- A capability needs roles, processes and an appropriate agile organization to come alive.

Key principles for defining roles and responsibilities

Each core capability area must be translated into the roles and responsibilities that are needed to build it. The translation of capabilities into roles can differ between organizations. Every role refers to a set of competencies that a person who takes on this role should have and a number of responsibilities that the role should be able to fulfil. For each role there is a chapter head who ensures that all employees that work in the role have the right level of skills, follow defined approaches and quality standards and share knowledge about methodologies and ensure reusability of artefacts across product teams. The overall steering is driven by CDOs, depending on the realm of decisions to be made, sometimes in a data and AI board organized by CDOs that should include the relevant senior business stakeholders.

KEY PRINCIPLES
Defining roles and responsibilities

- Each capability area must be translated into the roles and responsibilities needed to build it.
- Each role can support several capabilities and has a defined set of competencies and responsibilities.
- For every role, there are heads who ensure there are skills, approaches, quality standards and sharing in their chapter as required.
- New roles might be added depending on the evolving capability needs based on the data product strategy and the capability strategy.

Key principles for setting up the agile organization

A majority of traditional organizations fail to become truly agile organizations. To achieve velocity and ownership, it makes sense to put the different roles into small interdisciplinary product squad teams that actually focus on a set of data products in a particular data product domain. Several product squad teams can belong to one data product domain. Such squad teams usually should have at least one person for each type of role, ie data strategist, data product manager, data scientist. Typically, one of the data product managers leads the product squad team. The heads of each of the role families, eg head of machine learning and data science, might at the same time be placed in one of the teams. Everyone who has the same role would fall into the same chapter, eg all data scientists would be organized in the machine learning and data science chapter.

KEY PRINCIPLES
Setting up the agile organization

- To foster agility, teams should be cross-functional, dedicated, self-sufficient and empowered with a focus on business problems.

- A product domain is represented by one or more cross-functional product team 'squads', keeping team size below 10.

- For every data product domain, there is one experienced product manager appointed as the data product domain leader.

- Every product squad team in the data product domain is led by a data product manager with a direct reporting line to the data product domain leader.

- The types of roles needed in a product team can differ depending on the purpose of the team.

- All the product squad teams own a part of the product portfolio and are steering their portfolio and delivery and operations of data products in scope.

- Product squad teams should have a clear mission and all the capabilities that are required to solve the business problems defined in the mission.

Key principles for implementing and adapting processes

Finally, core and supporting processes need to ensure that data product teams are orchestrated where and when required. The goal is to deliver the data and AI strategy in the most effective way.

KEY PRINCIPLES
Implementing and adapting processes

- Manage the data product lifecycle processes.
- Provide overarching demand management and portfolio steering and prioritization of resources when there are conflicts and unplanned demands.
- Steer and prioritize the work of the data infrastructure team that is needed by all data product teams.
- Ensure data governance is organized and executed across the organization with a focus on making data available, understandable, usable and trustworthy.
- Make the rest of the organization more compatible, which could require, for example, adapting purchasing, legal, security, compliance, IT and finance processes to better support an agile delivery and management approach.

Determining core capabilities for data and AI

There are a number of core capabilities that are needed for driving digital transformation through data and AI. There will be further capabilities that are not covered here that need to be added based on the individual requirements of your data product strategy and these need to be determined. Each core capability is described in terms of purpose, responsibilities and connected roles in the following.

CHECKLIST

Core capabilities for data and AI:

- strategy and transformation;
- product management and user experience;

- machine learning and data science;
- data engineering, infrastructure and architecture;
- data management, quality and governance;
- backend and frontend software engineering;
- data analytics and business intelligence.

Strategy and transformation

Designing and implementing a data and AI strategy is not a one-time activity, but an ongoing recursive process that regularly needs to be checked and revised. It is needed to manage, steer and monitor overall resources and stakeholders in the data and AI programme to ensure that the product, capability and change strategy are successfully implemented. It includes the development of the product, capability and change strategy and portfolio, and setting and monitoring metrics for the data and AI transformation as a whole, as presented in Chapter 2. The main alignment between senior stakeholders is managed via the data and AI board, which will be explained later. The most important role to fulfil this capability is the chief data officer.

Product management and user experience

Each data product that is part of the product strategy and portfolio needs to be managed along its entire lifecycle. It all starts with finding and prioritizing the right product ideas. Then, the data product needs to be designed, which includes the definition of the scope and roadmap, the design of the user experience and user journey, the verification of the suitability of the data for the data product, the estimation of the business impact, the design of the initial solution architecture and the handling of ethical and compliance challenges with regard to the data product (see also Chapter 3). The most promising ideas are validated and then further developed and deployed as minimum viable product to be piloted and later scaled (see Chapter 4). Once in operation, change requests and new releases need to be managed and the data product has to be monitored and maintained.

Machine learning and data science

The higher the data maturity of an organization, the more likely it is that there are machine learning models at the core of data products. Machine learning and data science starts with understanding the business problem that should be solved by the data product and translating it into a data science problem statement, which is often a mathematical representation of the business problem and therefore forces a much higher level of precision in the problem statement. For example, if the business problem is to understand why customers are churning, the data science problem might be to identify features that correlate with customers who have not bought a product for more than a year. The next step for a data scientist is to get access to datasets that contain the raw data to create features and target variables for the data science problem and understanding how data fields should be interpreted. For instance, a column in a table called 'number of customer complaints' could be tied to one particular channel, eg phone calls, and not counting customer complaints on other channels, eg website or email. Not knowing exactly how to interpret data can lead to major mistakes during the modelling process and the interpretation of the model. Therefore, interviews with data and business domain experts are an absolute necessity, especially when the data scientists have not used the datasets before. An exploratory data analysis helps individuals to get familiar with the dataset, for example, by looking at the data types and minimum, maximum and average values of each column and their distributions. Datasets in most cases contain raw data that needs to be cleaned, integrated and prepared before the actual machine learning models can be created. The target variable for the machine learning models is of particular importance. Raw data often needs to be condensed into more meaningful features for the machine learning models. For example, instead of having individual sales transactions of a customer as an input, features that could be calculated are the average basket size, the frequency of purchases and average time between purchases. A central activity is then the actual modelling, which aims to find the best machine learning model type (eg random forest, linear regression, neural network) and calibrate it to best predict the target variable using the input features. The best model is then applied to a part of the dataset that was withheld and not used during training, the test dataset, to check if the model is generalizable. Once a good model has been found, it is tweaked and optimized and then ready for deployment and operation.

Data engineering, infrastructure and architecture

A machine learning model usually cannot by itself provide much value if it is not supplied with fresh data on a regular basis and if its output cannot be further used by other systems. It also needs to run somewhere on a data platform, and somebody needs to develop and operate the data platform and the data lake that is built as part of the data platform. After the data product is developed, it has to be deployed on the data platform, typically by building and operating CI/CD pipelines that automate the process and automated software tests support the reliability of the deployments. The incoming data streams need to be pre-processed in a production environment, which is typically done manually by the data scientist during validation, but which needs to be automated for production. The entire data platform and all data products have to be monitored after the go live to ensure that they are working. All these tasks require data engineers, which makes them very precious resources that are in high demand.

Data management, quality and governance

Building data products relies heavily on high-quality data that is understandable, accessible and usable from a legal perspective. Data management and governance are therefore crucial to managing the data lake, adding new sources and dealing with access requests correctly. Moreover, for data to become trustworthy, data quality rules should be defined that are monitored and tracked. Data in the data lake can only be used properly if it is well described in a data catalogue and there is good metadata on what the data contains and where it comes from. Not all data can be used for all purposes, and there are many legal, regulatory, ethical and compliance restrictions on how data can actually be used. Particularly in structured SQL databases and data warehouses, data models need to be defined to create a common structure of tables and relationships between the tables, which can be especially challenging when data is integrated from several sources. Finally, there are often missing pieces in the data due to some data not being captured at all or the customer's consent not being sufficiently managed, which requires special attention and proactive involvement to mitigate and improve.

Backend and frontend software engineering

Machine learning models are difficult to use in business processes if they are not wrapped with frontend and backend software that allow a business problem to be addressed holistically. Most data products therefore consist of frontend and backend functionalities besides the data processing and machine learning functionalities. Usually, it starts with translating user needs to functionality requirements and designing those functionalities by defining and prioritizing features into a backlog. Using agile sprints, the features are implemented, tested and deployed. Oftentimes, Scrum is used as the agile method for development, which includes formats such as retrospectives, sprint reviews and sprint planning on a regular basis, eg weekly, biweekly or monthly. Finally, deployed functionalities need to be operated and maintained and new features can be added to improve the data product.

Data analytics and business intelligence

Not all data products need to contain machine learning models; they can also have descriptive analytics in the form of standard reports and dashboards and possibilities for self-service business intelligence as the main output. Besides, in many cases, data products that do focus on machine learning come along with a dashboard which enables the results of the machine learning model to be monitored and tracked more easily for the business departments. Usually, an important mission of data analytics is to define metrics for the business and leading financial figures and integrate these in dashboards and reports. It can also include the set-up of self-service tools for business intelligence, such as, for example, Power BI, Tableau or Qlik, that allow business users to conduct their own analyses. Since metrics and financial reporting regularly require a very high standard of quality and reliability, data analytics often sets requirements for data management and data integration. All dashboards, reporting and self-service tools have to be operated and supported.

Defining roles and responsibilities to implement capabilities

Archetypal roles that have been discussed before are described in detail in this section with a definition of the role, its relevance and connected responsibilities as well as the respective skill requirements.

Chief data officer

The most senior data-related role in the organization is the chief data officer (the role – as all other roles – can have different names, for example, chief data and analytics officer or VP data). Depending on the data maturity of the organization and the importance of data for the industry, this role usually sits either on the board or one or two levels below the board. Therefore, this role is a senior or executive management position and requires a lot of leadership experience and skills on top of a deep understanding of data, analytics and AI, software and platform engineering and architecture, and the business strategy of the corporation.

ROLE DEFINITION: CHIEF DATA OFFICER

Purpose: Ensure that data and AI transformation works as a whole.

Capability area: Data and AI strategy and transformation.

Responsibilities:

- Set strategy of entire data and AI transformation.
- Monitor progress of data and AI transformation with metrics.

- Make investments and steer resources for data and AI transformation.
- Organize the data and AI board and manage key stakeholders.
- Change management and education.

Data product manager

Data product managers are true multi-talents in data science and management. They hold the end-to-end responsibility for the data products. The data and AI product manager works closely with the data scientists and data engineers, but also speaks the language of more traditional business functions. They possess domain knowledge on the business side, but ideally have hands-on-experience in data science or software development and a strong technical intuition. All the decisions related to the data and AI product converge on this role, which requires excellent communication and negotiation skills, a leadership and entrepreneurial personality and a knack for organization and stakeholder management. They are the key managers to bring change within your organization and help create a cultural bridge between the traditional and the digital part of the corporation.

ROLE DEFINITION: DATA PRODUCT MANAGER

Purpose: Manage each data product that is part of the product strategy and portfolio along its lifecycle from idea to operations.

Capability area: Product management and user experience.

Responsibilities:

- Manage the data product during its entire lifecycle.
- Identify product ideas.
- Design the product and its user experience.
- Validate the idea for a data product.
- Manage the development and deployment of the MVP of the data product.

- Gather change requests for the data product when it is in production.
- Coordinate ethics and legal topics for data and AI.
- Manage development teams.
- Manage stakeholders for data products.

Data scientist

Data scientists (also known as machine learning engineers) proto-type, build and operate machine learning models. The role of the data scientist has evolved over the last few years from a clear focus on business understanding, data preparation, data analysis, statistics and machine learning to a role that requires more and more complex software engineering skills by using Python not only for data science, but also as a programming language that focuses on deploying and operating machine learning models. This reflects the shift from proof of concepts to data products that actually bring value to a wider breadth of the organization. Data scientists need to build a strong business domain knowledge in the domain for which they build machine learning models. Due to the higher focus on operationaliza-tion and deployment of data scientists, managing relationships with the business departments within the domains is mostly done by the data product manager role. The data scientist needs to have strong quantitative skills and an understanding of statistics and machine learning models as well as programming skills.

ROLE DEFINITION: DATA SCIENTIST

Purpose: Create and run machine learning models.

Capability area: Machine learning and data science.

Responsibilities:

- Translate the business problem into a data science problem statement.
- Check data suitability.
- Conduct exploratory data analysis.

- Prepare data for machine learning.
- Train and test machine learning models.
- Deploy machine learning models.
- Operate machine learning models.

Data engineer

In contrast to data scientists, data engineers are less involved in data-related topics and more in the technical architecture and software that are wrapped around the machine learning model to automate its deployment and operations and make the results usable to business users. Once the analytical model is developed, the main focus shifts from machine learning model development to software and architecture development. Data engineers therefore play a more prominent role than data scientists after prototyping. Many companies have hired a lot of data scientists and not enough data engineers. Data engineers need a wide range of skills, which can vary quite a lot depending on the particular role requirements. Key skills are developing backend software, designing and implementing the architecture of the data platform and of data product solutions, connecting and integrating different data sources and creating data pipelines and APIs and bringing data products into production.

ROLE DEFINITION: DATA ENGINEER

Purpose: Enable the deployment and operation of data products.

Capability area: Data engineering, infrastructure and architecture.

Responsibilities:

- Create input and output data pipelines and interfaces to other systems.
- Manage the technical infrastructure of the data lake.
- Develop and implement the solution and platform architecture.
- Design CI/CD pipelines and deploy data products.
- Operate the data products and the platform.
- Test the overall data product.

Data manager

Data is the critical resource for machine learning and artificial intelligence. Managing this critical resource is a discipline in itself and requires the special attention of a dedicated role, the role of the data manager. Data managers take care of ensuring that the right data is captured and made available via the data lake. They are responsible for all processes around data including data capture, data governance, data models, data quality and implementing effective data protection. The role can be more technically focused on data profiling, data integration and metadata management or more managerially focused on data governance and quality processes, depending on the particular requirements of the organization.

ROLE DEFINITION: DATA MANAGER

Purpose: Ensure that data is usable, trustable and available.

Capability area: Data management, quality and governance.

Responsibilities:

- Manage data platform and acquisitions of new data sources.
- Manage access rights to data.
- Create and implement data quality monitoring rules.
- Define and enforce processes for data protection and data compliance.
- Manage data catalogue and surrounding processes to collect metadata.
- Define and manage data models.
- Identify gaps in data collection and customer consent management.

Software developer

Backend and frontend developers are roles that appear more and more frequently in data organizations that have shifted from a project to a product paradigm. Backends and frontends are often an important part of solving end-to-end business problems. When a machine learning algorithm automates a process, backend software functionality is usually needed to execute the process and frontend software functionality is built to administer, configure and monitor the machine learning algorithm. Effective software developers are able to understand the business problem and translate it with the help of the data product manager into backend and frontend requirements and create well-documented production-ready software code that is automatically tested and deployed. They are also responsible for operating and maintaining the software.

ROLE DEFINITION: SOFTWARE DEVELOPER

Purpose: Build backend and frontend software to make data products usable in operational business processes.

Capability area: Backend and frontend software engineering.

Responsibilities:

- Translate user needs to functionality requirements.
- Design backend and frontend functionalities.
- Implement backend and frontend functionalities.
- Test and deploy backend and frontend functionalities.
- Operate, maintain and extend backend and frontend functionalities.

Data analyst

Data analysts are the business intelligence experts within the data team. They design reports and dashboards and support their implementation. How useful data insights can be is very much dependent on the skill of the data analysts in visualizing results in a way that users find easy to understand and interpret and integrate into their workflows. Data analysts should have strong skills in quantitative analysis, communication and design, with (ideally) basic data science and programming skills in (usually) JavaScript and Python. They should be experts in self-service business intelligence and dashboard tools, such as, for example, Tableau, Qlik, Looker or Power BI. They should also be able to draw detailed mock-ups after an analysis of user needs using mock-up software tools (eg Balsamiq, Mockingbird or Framer X) and be comfortable in operating and supporting dashboards they create.

ROLE DEFINITION: DATA ANALYST

Purpose: Create dashboards and reports that reflect in metrics and financial figures how well the business is functioning.

Capability area: Data analytics.

Responsibilities:

- Define how to measure the most important metrics in the organization.
- Design dashboards and self-service environments for business intelligence.
- Build standard reports that are provided to decision-makers, operational managers, financial controllers and regulators.
- Create dashboards to monitor the performance of machine learning models.
- Set requirements for data management and integration.
- Operate business intelligence solutions.

Each of the roles brings unique skills into a data team that, combined, enable an organization to design, validate, build, deploy and operate data products effectively. The next section looks at how the different skills can best be put together.

Setting up the agile organization

Oftentimes, the biggest discussion point when setting up organizations is the question of where roles should be placed. Intrinsically, business and IT departments argue that data roles should be placed into their departments and not somewhere else, as each department continuously fights for more resources, relevance and power. Questions that frequently arise during such discussions are:

- Should teams be staffed cross-functionally or based on their roles?
- What leadership positions are there?
- Which roles should be placed in business and which in IT?
- Should roles be spread throughout business departments, units and markets, or should they be more centralized at headquarters?

There are no right or wrong answers to these questions; many different ways can be equally successful and each organization requires different approaches depending on the situation and context. There are, however, some principles to build agile organizations that can work as guidance irrespective of the specific situation organizations are in, which are presented in the following. These principles can help structure the discussion and set the focus on abandoning the working mode known in traditional corporates. They also facilitate the adoption of an agile working mode that forms the basis of company processes fostered by global digital players.

The limitations of traditional organizational set-ups

The most straightforward way to set up data and AI teams for a chief data and analytics officer is to hire the heads of each role (eg head of data science, head of data engineering, head of data management) and to create teams based on the roles under them – a data science team, a data engineering team, a data management team, etc. Many organizations start their data journey in exactly this way. The main challenge with such an organizational set-up is that it requires a lot of planning coordination to ensure that the right roles are available in projects to deliver data products. Usually, a lot of conflicts come up with regard to the prioritization of resources, and effectively new silos are created. A data science team might start to complain about the data product management team as they do not properly document what needs to be done and do not ensure that data comes well documented. The data product management team might quickly be fed up with the data science team refusing to work on data products before they are sufficiently defined and understood, although they need their support to properly define the data products during ideation. Data product managers care about their products, data scientists about their models, data managers about their data and data engineers about their solution architecture. In this organizational set-up, nobody really cares about solving the entire business problem that a data product intends to solve.

Organizing teams in cross-functional product squads and role-based chapters

A key learning for organizations that strive to become more agile is that teams should actually be cross-functional, dedicated, self-sufficient, and empowered with a focus on business problems. Equally important to where to place data teams is how to organize them. There are two traditional ways of organizing them. The first way is to put everyone with the same role organizationally into one team, eg all data scientists into the data science team, and staffing people of different roles into cross-functional project teams. The disadvantage is that project teams dissolve once the project is over. The second way is to divide people up across departments that focus on a particular business domain and having mixed roles in the departments. Here, the problem can be similar to the challenges of a decentralized approach described above: employees that fulfil the data roles might not get enough support to develop their skills. A popular approach in agile software engineering is to combine the two ways in a unified approach that has been pioneered by Spotify successfully and adopted by many other organizations.[1] A squad is a small cross-functional team of three to nine people that is self-organized and has a long-term mission. It has the autonomy to decide what to build, how to build it and how to work together under certain constraints and rules set by the company. It aligns with regard to the product strategy, the priorities of the company and with what other squad teams do. The focus on a long-term mission allows the squad members to become true experts in the business domain they focus on, while the mix of roles ensures that the squad team can solve business problems that require a wide range of different skills. To ensure that people that share the same role can support each other, chapters for each role are established that set standards for their roles and share knowledge and best practices. Squads with interconnected missions can form a tribe that has up to 100 people and a joint set of priorities and resulting budget allocations. The Spotify model allows the creation of cross-functional product squads in each data product domain of the data product strategy, while building up skills in each chapter, which represent the different roles and core capabilities of the capability strategy. Figure 5.2 shows an example of an interdisciplinary squad and chapter set-up.

FIGURE 5.2 Example set-up of an agile cross-functional data and AI organization

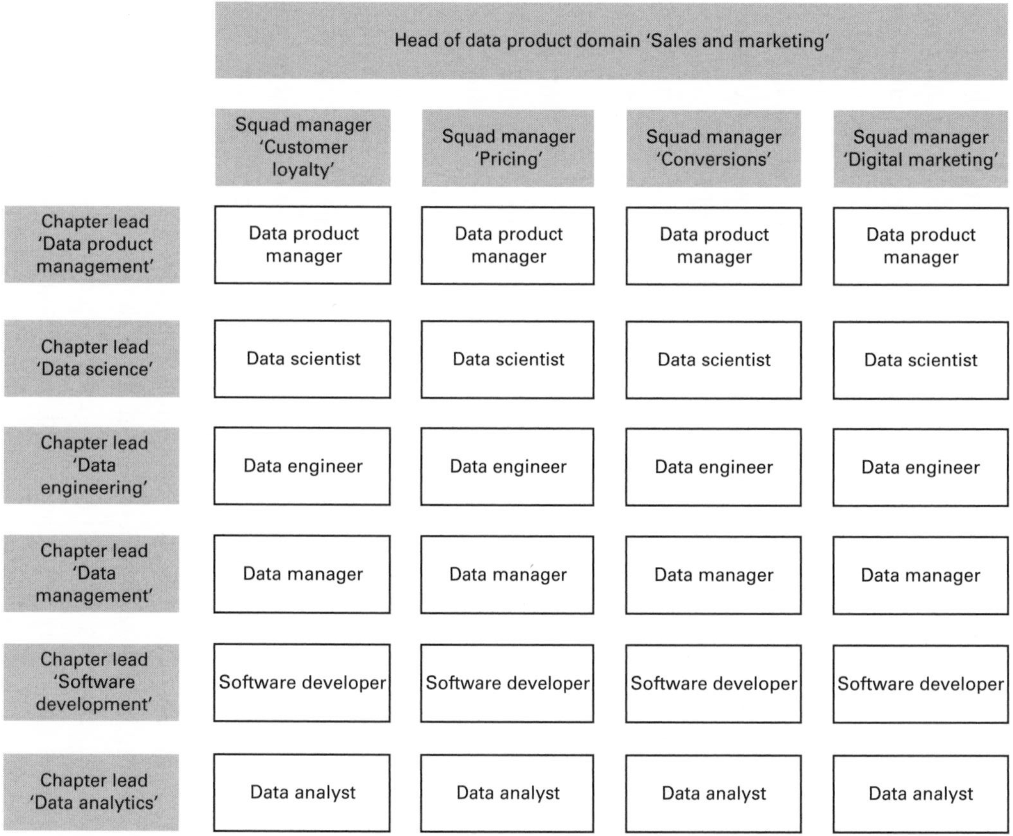

	Head of data product domain 'Sales and marketing'			
	Squad manager 'Customer loyalty'	Squad manager 'Pricing'	Squad manager 'Conversions'	Squad manager 'Digital marketing'
Chapter lead 'Data product management'	Data product manager	Data product manager	Data product manager	Data product manager
Chapter lead 'Data science'	Data scientist	Data scientist	Data scientist	Data scientist
Chapter lead 'Data engineering'	Data engineer	Data engineer	Data engineer	Data engineer
Chapter lead 'Data management'	Data manager	Data manager	Data manager	Data manager
Chapter lead 'Software development'	Software developer	Software developer	Software developer	Software developer
Chapter lead 'Data analytics'	Data analyst	Data analyst	Data analyst	Data analyst

KEY PRINCIPLES
Building the agile and cross-functional data and AI organization

Data product domain team:

- mission and OKRs defined as part of the data product strategy;
- led by a data product domain leader;
- consist of one or more squad teams (see below).

Squad team (based on data product domains):

- mission to build data products within one business domain;
- cross-functional team of three to nine people;
- self-organized under consideration of overarching priorities;
- team members work in different roles;
- might have their own sub OKRs.

Chapter (based on roles):

- All employees that work in a role belong to the chapter corresponding to this role, eg data product management chapter, data science chapter, data engineering chapter...
- Chapter leads set standards for their discipline that everyone in the role needs to follow and provide training and knowledge sharing opportunities.

What are the leadership positions in data and AI?

Besides the chief data and analytics officer, there are three types of leadership roles. There are leaders for each data product domain and squad managers for each squad team inside a data product domain, and leaders for each role-based chapter. Data product domain leaders and squad managers focus on direct business outcomes through designing and delivering great data products, while the chapter leaders aim to build great capabilities. Data product domain leaders manage all product squads that belong to a particular data product domain. Squad managers usually have a direct reporting line to their respective data product domain leaders and manage the cross-functional squad. Each squad contains members that work in different roles and do not need to have a direct reporting line to the squad manager. Chapter leads manage everyone who is in the same role. As a good practice, we recommend having both chapter leads and squad managers as they take care of two different things. In smaller companies, the level of squad manager might not exist and squads are directly managed by the data product domain leader.

The collaboration between business and IT

A similar frequently asked question is if data roles should be placed in IT or business. The answer probably lies in the middle, as digital transformation blurs the line between the two. Business and IT should work integrated in a joint virtual organization following agile approaches such as Scrum and Kanban. It is advisable in organizations that have a strong split between business and IT to create a joint data unit that has a business and an IT leader with the same common management goals. Some roles should definitely be on the business side. This is particularly true for the role of the chief data officer and data product managers, as both determine business strategy for data, analytics and AI and steer business budgets to build and operate data products. Data scientists, data managers and data analysts are roles that are more business centric, while data engineers and software developers can be seen as roles that are more IT centric, although this divide is more flexible and should be adjusted based on the individual requirements in the organization

Centralization versus decentralization of data roles

There are four ways of placing data teams in the organization. The first one is to put all data roles in a central unit. This is a valid option for companies that are just starting with their data journey, as skills can be grown more easily and it avoids unsynchronized investments, but it has the major disadvantage that skills are not available across the business units where the business value is actually created. The second option is quite the opposite: spreading all data roles across the business units. This usually results in data scientists tackling the most relevant business problems in their business domain as they work very closely with the business. Also, the acceptance of data products is increased as everyone is in the same team. On the downside, data scientists and data engineers are completely spread across the enterprise and might not be able to support each other. It might also lead to a lack of responsibility for overarching cross-functional data topics, such as building and running a joint data platform, or the same investments might be done twice, leading to duplicate efforts. A hybrid model known as the 'hub and spoke' between a centralized data team and decentral teams close to core business processes is currently seen as the best practice. While there is an overarching strategy, quality and role standards and a central data platform and operations, data science work is usually done close to the business processes that data products aim to support. This model aims to navigate between central and decentral steering. Departmental politics and alignment between departments are probably the most important challenge, as the right balance between central and decentral needs to be found every day, topic by topic. Setting strategic guidelines that set the expectations of what should be done centrally or decentrally can therefore be of huge benefit to avoid unnecessary conflicts, which hinder implementation progress.

Why centralize data roles?

- Good at the start as skills can easily be developed.
- More coordinated investments in data platform and data enablers.
- Aligned strategy with synergies across business departments.

Why decentralize data roles?

- Higher acceptance of data products.
- Easier to identify relevant business problems to work on.
- Data scientists gain business domain knowledge faster.

Which steering bodies are needed for data and AI?

Depending on the size of the organization, there can be a number of different committees for data and AI. The highest management body is the data and AI board, which should be positioned at C-level and which makes the most important strategic investment, governance and prioritization decisions with regard to data infrastructure, data architecture, data governance and the data product portfolio. In medium sized organizations, the data and AI board usually is the management board. Below the data and AI board, a number of working groups can work on particular data domains or other specific data topics such as, for example, data architecture. The data and AI board is usually organized by CDOs.

There are some great practices for designing agile data and AI organizations. This section outlined some of them and explored their strengths and weaknesses. Independent of the organizational structure chosen, a number of processes need to be established, which will be examined in the next section.

Implementing and adapting processes

The final element remaining for the organization of data and AI after sorting out core capabilities, roles and responsibilities, and the agile organization, is the implementation of processes for data and AI. There are four core process areas (see Figure 5.3) that need to be implemented and adapted for data and AI:

1 **Data product lifecycle processes** to design, develop, deploy and operate data products.

2 **Data and AI governance processes** to ensure that data is captured, processed and provided with high quality and made usable, understandable and trustable and that machine learning models are explainable, trustable, controllable and compliant.

3 **Data platform processes** to develop, operate and maintain the data platform.

4 **Other processes** for purchasing, recruitment, performance evaluation, legal and compliance approvals and for investments need to be adapted and changed to better support the data and AI organization.

Data product lifecycle processes

Chapters 3 and 4 addressed in detail how data products can be managed effectively throughout their lifecycle. At the beginning, ideas for data product candidates are created in an ideation phase. Each data product candidate goes through an initial assessment phase that estimates the feasibility and value of the data product and its fit with regard to the data product strategy. The top evaluated data product ideas are further defined in terms of features covered, business impact, user experience, technical feasibility, and ethics and compliance and then validated in a proof of concept. If everything goes well and business value, user acceptance, compliance and feasibility can be validated, the minimum viable product is designed, implemented and deployed to production. Before go live, the current business processes often need to be redesigned to make full use of the new data product. Users are trained in how best to use the data product and how their adapted business process works. Once in production, a data product

FIGURE 5.3 Processes for data and AI

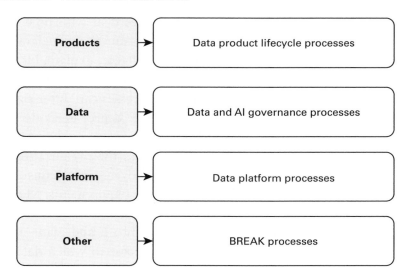

is operated and monitored, further developed into the final product and maintained. Some data products can be scaled to further scopes, eg from one factory location to many other factory locations. The data product manager is responsible for the data product from the beginning to the end of the data product lifecycle.

CHECKLIST

Types of product lifecycle processes:

- identifying and prioritizing the need for a data product;
- evaluating data product ideas to add to the product portfolio;
- designing the data product;
- validating the data product;
- developing the data product;
- deploying the data product;
- operating and maintaining the data product;
- scaling the data product.

Data and AI governance processes

The second set of processes for data and AI are governance processes, which will be covered as part of technology and governance in Chapter 6. Data and AI governance processes deal with how data and AI can be used across the organization and aim to make data and AI more accessible, trustable, usable, controllable, explainable and compliant. Data managers are the central employees for data and AI governance processes. The scope of these processes can differ significantly between organizations, and is to a large degree dependent on the data maturity and ambition. More and more organizations aim to democratize the usage of data assets across the organization by making data available and usable to all employees under consideration of the restrictions of legal and regulatory requirements. Making data available can be achieved by establishing a central data lake with the most important data being loaded into it and made available. Data access processes steer who gets access to which data for which purposes. To ensure a higher quality of data, data quality monitoring rules can be implemented when data is loaded into the data lake. Data models that define the most important master and transactional data, and data catalogues that document the data in the data lake make data easier to use for analytics and machine learning. Data collection and customer consent processes are applied when data is not yet gathered or the customer consent has not been collected to enable capturing and usage of data. Finally, ethics and regulation in AI make it necessary to ensure that machine learning models can be trusted and that they act according to legal and regulatory requirements and according to company values.

CHECKLIST

Types of data and AI governance processes:

- establishing AI governance to create trust in AI-based decision-making;
- managing data platform and acquisitions of new data sources;
- managing access rights to data;
- creating and implementing data quality monitoring rules;
- defining and enforcing processes for data protection and data compliance;
- managing data catalogue and surrounding processes to collect metadata;
- defining and managing data models;
- identifying gaps in data collection and customer consent management.

Data platform processes

Steering the development and operations of the data platform is the third set of processes and is also covered in Chapter 6 on technology and governance. Demands for new platform features arise from the data portfolio, capability and change strategies as well as more specifically from the data products that it is planned will be built and the data governance processes that are established or extended in scope. Data engineers are the key personnel for all DevOps and MLOps processes related to the data platform. The typical platform engineering team has a full backlog until the year 2525. The consequence is that demand needs to be prioritized in a way that best supports the overall data and AI strategy. Priorities set in the data product, capability and transformation strategies should be directly reflected in the demand prioritization of the data platform team. New data platform features have to be designed, implemented and deployed while maintaining the stability of the entire data platform and the products already running on the platform. The data platform has to be constantly operated, supported, monitored and maintained. Last but not least, the data platform should regularly undergo security and architecture assessments, resulting in increased monitoring capabilities and improvements of the overall technical and security architecture. Potential changes to reduce complexity and increase standardization of the data platform should be regularly identified and implemented.

CHECKLIST

Types of data platform processes:

- collecting and prioritizing the demands for platform features;
- designing data platform features;
- developing data platform features;
- deploying data platform features;
- operating, monitoring and maintaining the data platform;
- security assessment, monitoring and enhancement of the data platform;
- architecture assessment, monitoring and enhancement of the data platform.

BREAK processes

It is likely that a range of processes already exist in the company that affect the management of data products, data governance and data platform. These processes often need to be changed or adapted to fit the needs of the agile data and AI organization better. They include at least the five BREAK processes: buy, recruit, evaluate, approve, kill. If one of these processes is not working, it can break all other processes.

- The first process is the **buy** process. A major problem in data and AI projects is that most purchasing processes in large corporations simply take too long. Purchasing and introducing new software can take more than a year, and getting the right suppliers on board can be similarly challenging. Adapting buying processes to allow collaboration with startups and smaller suppliers faster and use software as a service from marketplaces such as those provided by Amazon Web Services can increase the speed and quality of delivery of data products significantly.

- The second process is adapting the **recruiting** process. Acquiring talent for data and AI can be similarly challenging. Corporate hiring processes often lack the flexibility to provide offers to talents that are in high demand on the market.

- The third process handles the way performance is **evaluated** in traditional companies. This can be a disadvantage for tech staff in comparison to management staff. There needs to be a clear and attractive career path for developers and machine learning engineers.

- The fourth process deals with the way legal and compliance **approvals** are given before, during and after data product development. A dedicated compliance and legal support is usually needed to ensure that valuable data and AI developers are not standing in line and waiting for months to get the approvals to start their work and wasting their valuable resource.

- Eventually, a key principle for data product lifecycle management is that high-impact ideas for data products can be quickly validated in terms of feasibility and user experience and that data product ideas that are not performing well are taken out of the product portfolio as quickly as possible. As a consequence, the fifth process is the **kill** process, which is often a major change in how most companies operate. Finance and project management processes should become more flexible to allow this rapid trial-and-error mode.

The adaptation of these processes is typically a major change management project by itself and requires a lot of senior executive support and attention, and it can take quite a while for changes to be truly implemented.

CHECKLIST

The BREAK processes:

- **B**uy: How to purchase software and services in agile data and AI teams.
- **R**ecruit: How to acquire and keep great talent for data and AI.
- **E**valuate: How to measure performance in data and AI.
- **A**pprove: How to get legal and compliance approvals for data and AI.
- **K**ill: How to invest in a 'succeed fast/fail fast' mode in data and AI.

Lessons learned and pitfalls for capabilities and agile organization

Data and AI transformation need full business and IT involvement

It is easy to make the mistake of creating a data and AI organization on either the business or the IT side or where one side clearly dominates. All these options can create major problems. Without or with insufficient IT involvement, existing IT systems and databases cannot be connected to the data platform and machine learning applications cannot feed back the outputs of the algorithms to the operational systems. A lack of business involvement, on the other hand, usually results in a focus on the technical aspects of data and AI while ignoring the fact that data and AI are actually part of a significant business transformation. Finding the right mix of business and IT involvement in the data and AI transformation is therefore key. One way to achieve this is to have a business leader and an IT leader that operate under the same joint goals. Having the business and IT data teams physically co-located and working in an integrated way is equally important to ensure that no barriers are created that hinder collaboration and innovation from taking place.

Provide room for self-organized teams with a strong alignment between the teams

Squad teams that determine to a large degree what they do to fulfil their missions is for many organizations something really new, and challenges long-standing paradigms. In most cases, it is not compatible with how the company is steered and therefore budget rounds and reviews need to be set up in a way that gives squad teams the autonomy they need. A first step is to align on missions for squad teams that have a buy-in of all senior stakeholders and which are derived from the corporate strategy and the product portfolio strategy. Furthermore, boundaries should be established in which the squad teams can and need to operate and which make it easier for the other parts of the company to interact with the squad and set expectations. These boundaries are defined by senior executives, the data and AI strategy, budgetary limits for the squad teams, the overarching data product roadmap and architectural requirements that squad teams need to commit to. Squad teams have to align with other squad teams to ensure that different data products can fit together into the overall target picture.

Start small and grow continuously

Starting with too-large squads or too many squad teams at the same time can be very challenging. There is a high risk that squad teams become ineffective. A good practice is to start a new squad with at least a product manager, a data scientist and a data engineer and then to gradually increase the team size by adding more of these roles or other roles depending on the mission of the squad. Also, it usually makes sense to begin with one squad per data product domain and one squad that is dedicated to developing and operating the data platform. Processes and standards need to be developed that are adapted across the squads. This is where the chapters come into play. Having chapter leads early on is therefore as important as naming squad managers. When further squads are established, chapter leads will train the new squad managers to adhere to the guidelines and standards to ensure that the ramp-up of the new squad goes as smooth as possible.

Checklist for capabilities and agile organization

The following checklist covers the four phases of capabilities and agile organization, and can be used to verify whether any important aspects have been missed out.

CHECKLIST

Core capabilities:

- strategy and transformation;
- product management and user experience;
- machine learning and data science;
- data engineering, infrastructure and architecture;
- data management, quality and governance;
- backend and frontend software engineering;
- data analytics and business intelligence.

Roles and responsibilities:

- chief data officer;
- data product manager;
- data scientist;
- data engineer;
- data manager;
- software developer;
- data analyst.

Setting up the agile organization:

- cross-functional squad teams organized by data product domain;
- role-based chapters;
- integration of business and IT;
- balance of central and decentral roles;
- data and AI board established.

Implementing and adapting core processes:

- data product lifecycle processes;
- data and AI governance processes;
- data platform processes;
- BREAK processes (buy, recruit, evaluate, approve, kill).

Summary and conclusion

Organizations need to build a number of core capabilities to be able to deliver data products. This requires the introduction of many potentially new roles and responsibilities and business processes, and an agile organizational set-up. Core capabilities additionally need the right technologies and governance, which are covered in the next chapter.

Note

1 Kniberg, H, Spotify engineering culture (part 1) [Blog] Spotify R&D, 27 March 2014. https://engineering.atspotify.com/2014/03/27/spotify-engineering-culture-part-1/ (archived at https://perma.cc/F9YW-EZA8)

06

Technology and governance

LEARNING OBJECTIVES FOR THIS CHAPTER

- Learn how to design the data platform.
- Learn how to build the data infrastructure and create central data repositories.
- Learn how to set up architecture and development standards for machine learning, business intelligence and data products.
- Learn how to establish effective data and AI governance.
- Learn how to ensure that machine learning models can be trusted.
- Learn why it is better to build the data platform on a public cloud infrastructure.
- Learn why you should document everything related to the architecture of your data product.

Key principles for technology and governance

So far, this book has mostly dealt with strategy, organization and data product delivery and management. While all of these things are elementary to succeeding in data and AI, the basis for being able to do any proper work is a well-functioning data platform and architecture and the governance of data and AI. Now, it is finally time to turn to technology and governance. More precisely, this chapter provides guidelines, processes and tactics on how best to implement the data platform and architecture and establish the data and AI governance in your organization in three phases. The data platform is the central place to acquire, manage, transform and provide data to data products and data consumers in the organization. It can be treated as an own data product domain, which justifies dedicating an entire product squad team to the data platform. Processes for collecting, prioritizing, designing, developing, deploying, operating, monitoring and maintaining data platform features should be managed in a similar way to other data products.

The data platform is where data is managed and provided for building data products and where data products can be run. The architecture provides a technological framework and governs how things happen on the data platform. Governance is needed to control the effective usage of data and AI.

FIGURE 6.1 The three phases of technology and governance

Technology and governance can be approached in three phases:

1 **Building the data platform:** Where and how data should be loaded, transformed, stored and provided to data consumers.

2 **Setting up the architecture and development standards:** How data products should be built on the data platform, and the tools and technologies to be used for machine learning and business intelligence.

3 **Implementing data and AI governance:** How data and AI are made accessible, trustable, controllable and understandable.

Key principles for building the data platform

The first step is to establish a common data infrastructure with central data repositories that allow every person and every application to get fast access to relevant data. This is the centrepiece of the data platform, which should be treated as a separate data product domain area in its own right. It should also have a dedicated data platform team managed by the data platform squad manager and follow product management processes to design, prioritize and implement data product platform features. As the data platform should be highly performant, easily scalable and adaptable, a cloud infrastructure is currently the best choice for the underlying infrastructure of the data platform. Tools for moving, changing and managing data can make the life of the data platform team more stress-free and effective. The architecture of the data platform needs to be reviewed and constantly enhanced to keep it up to date and to assess and enhance security, cost efficiency, performance and stability.

KEY PRINCIPLES
Building the data platform

- Depending on the types of data, the right data storage needs to be selected.
- The data architecture can follow data warehouse or data lake principles.
- Data from source systems can be extracted via batch loads or streaming.
- Tools can support data engineers to extract, load, transform and manage data.
- A cloud-based data infrastructure environment offers flexibility and scalability.
- The architecture of the data platform should be regularly reviewed.

Key principles for setting up architecture and development standards

As the data organization and data product portfolio grows, so does the complexity of the solutions, the architecture and the data platform. If the complexity is not reduced whenever possible, it can easily become unmanageable. There are many ways to avoid unnecessary complexity in the data architecture by setting the right standards. The goal of standards for architecture and development should be to reduce complexity and increase the ease of building and operating reliable and compliant data products.

KEY PRINCIPLES
Setting up architecture and development standards

- Machine learning models should be deployed and operated in MLOps mode.

- Separate environments (stages) of the data platform should be used for validation, development, deployment and operation phases of data products.

- Microservice architecture standards should be followed.

- Data transformations are also software applications and can be treated with the same rules as other software code (eg version control, modularity).

- Programming languages and packages should be standardized to make collaboration more effectively used throughout all phases of data products.

- Technologies and tool standards for business intelligence and machine learning need to be defined considering different types of data users.

- Having the same toolbox and standards across the different stages of the data platform ensures that machine learning models are easier to deploy.

- A shared feature store and standardized metrics can accelerate the design and testing of machine learning models and business intelligence solutions.

Key principles for establishing data and AI governance

The most frequent product feature requests for the data platform are to connect new data sources containing highly demanded datasets to the data platform. The data on the data platform needs to be governed with regard to access rights, data quality, data protection security and compliance. When important data is missing, investigate whether the missing data can be somehow acquired or collected.

KEY PRINCIPLES
Establishing data and AI governance

- Trust for decision-making based on AI needs to be established by managing quality, transparency, explainability and control of machine learning algorithms.

- All relevant data sources in the organization should load data into the data platform on a frequent basis as raw data and integrated in a joint data model.
- Data access processes should be standardized and simplified to enable fast and compliant access for people and systems.
- Datasets should be described in a data catalogue and technical metadata gathered to understand where data comes from and what it contains.
- The data quality on the data platform should be managed, monitored, improved and corrected at source.
- Processes for data protection, security and compliance should be defined and enforced on the data platform in a user-friendly way.
- Data gaps in the data platform with high impact should be identified and actions defined to mitigate them on a regular basis.

Building the data platform

It has already been highlighted that the data platform is the central place to acquire, manage, transform and provide data to data products and data consumers in the organization and that it should be treated as an own data product domain with a dedicated product squad team. It was also mentioned that processes for collecting, prioritizing, designing, developing, deploying, operating, monitoring and maintaining data platform features should be managed in a similar way to how other data products are managed. In this section we will highlight a few important design decisions with regard to the types of data that should be managed, the data infrastructure that the data platform builds on, the storage technologies and architecture of the data platform and the way data is transferred and transformed between systems and the data platform.

STEPS FOR BUILDING THE DATA PLATFORM

1 Understand the different types of data.

2 Select the right data storage.

3 Design the data architecture.

4 Extract data from source systems.

5 Transform and load data.

6 Choose the data infrastructure environment.

Understanding the different types of data

In software development, defining what data types are required for the task at hand is one of the first steps when writing the first lines of code. Examples of data types include integer (whole number) and float (fractional numbers) for numbers, boolean (true or false), character and string for letters and words. Similarly, when laying out the plans for a data product, it is essential to understand the underlying types of data that are needed for the respective data product. This will form the basis for the other decisions related to data infrastructure. The main differentiation can be made among structured and unstructured data. An Excel spreadsheet is a typical example for structured data. By contrast, a Word file contains unstructured data, as it is not clear how the individual words and text passages relate to each other. Unstructured data cannot be easily reduced to one simple form like structured data, which makes their analysis much more complex. In between the two data types, there is semi-structured data that has a degree of hierarchy that makes handling it slightly easier than unstructured data. Examples include JSON and HTML files.

WHAT IS THE DIFFERENCE BETWEEN STRUCTURED AND UNSTRUCTURED DATA?

- **Structured data:** Structured data is highly organized, usually in the form of a table. A major advantage of structured data, apart from its clarity, is that the individual data points have well-defined relations to each other. For example, in an Excel spreadsheet it is usually clear that all the cells in one row are related to each other.

- **Unstructured data:** Unstructured data can be highly diverse and ranges from images to text files to web server logs to music files and many more. Pictures and videos are specific forms of unstructured data that are particularly difficult for machine learning models to process.

- **Semi-structured data:** Semi-structured data provides some form of structure while it is not as rigid as in structured data. For instance, a JSON file displays a hierarchical structure that reveals the respective relations of the individual hierarchy levels. Depending on the data format of the semi-structured data, the respective data storage types have to be chosen.

Selecting the right data storage

When the decision on the data type has been made, it is time to think about data storage technologies. Depending on the selected data type, the respective database model can be selected. The database model refers to the structure of the database that is used for data storage. If you have structured data, you will most likely choose a relational database model, because here data is organized in tables that have relations with each other. Examples for relational database management systems include MySQL, Oracle and PostgreSQL. You may have noticed that the term SQL has been mentioned several times in the context of relational database models. This is because SQL refers to structured query language and allows users to make specific and extensive queries and changes in a database with a simple and easy to understand syntax. Tables in the database can be readily added, joined, deleted and updated with a simple command for each operation in the table.

In contrast to relational database models, non-relational database models can manage the complexity of unstructured or semi-structured data. They are also called NoSQL database models, which means 'non-SQL' or 'not only SQL'. Since, as mentioned above, there is such a great variety of unstructured data, there are different categories of NoSQL database models that each cater for different types of unstructured data (see box above). The advantages of a NoSQL versus a relational database model, apart from its ability to deal with unstructured data, are its great flexibility and scalability. For a relational database model, you need to lay out a fixed schema that contains detailed information on which data and data types should be stored in the database before entering the first data point. A relational database model also reaches a natural barrier in terms of the complexity of the real world that it can display, because not all interdependencies between variables can be shown by interconnecting tables, even if the number of these tables is exceedingly large. NoSQL database models are better equipped to deal with the complexity of reality, since they can deal with unstructured data. The ever-increasing processing power of computer clusters allows for scaling data storage requirements that are needed for highly complex data products with a large amount of semi-structured or unstructured data. However, whether you choose a relational or non-relational database model depends on the respective use case. A clear-cut use case that handles structured data that has precise relations with each other and can be easily outlined in terms of a well-defined schema probably calls for a relational database model. See also Table 6.1 for more examples.

Designing the data architecture

Any company will typically use a number of different database systems, such as a database system for personnel data, another database system for product data, one for web server logs, and so forth. If you attempt to combine these different sources of data in the data platform, you will need to establish overarching data architecture. The two most common data architectures are the data warehouse architecture and the data lake. There is ample need for both architectures in a company, since there will be a number of use cases where relational databases are involved that can be well integrated into a data warehouse. At the same time, the rapidly increasing opportunities to collect and take advantage of unstructured data probably require a more flexible data lake architecture. The good news is that both architectures can coexist very well and, accordingly, both can be integrated into the data platform. Modern data platforms are often hybrids between data lakes and data warehouses. Finally, the architecture of the data platform should be regularly reviewed to assess and enhance security, cost efficiency, performance and stability.

TABLE 6.1 What are the differences between the four popular NoSQL database types?

NoSQL Database	Description	Use cases	Examples
Column-oriented	Data is stored by column rather than by row. This allows fast processing by SQL queries.	Usage of structured data and data warehouses (compare next section).	MariaDB, MonetDB, Apache Cassandra
Graph	Storing data as graphs that contain information on the relationships between people or items.	Suitable for use cases that emphasize relationships among entities, for instance in social networks or for fraud detection.	Neo4j, OrientDB, TigerGraph
Key value	A specific key can be associated with any type of value (eg document, text, number, etc). Queries are possible to a very limited extent only.	Useful when speed and scalability is required, eg when peaks have to be handled. Examples include web caches and real-time analyses.	Redis, Oracle Berkeley DB, Amazon DynamoDB
Document store	This is a specific type of key value database. A specific key is associated with different types of mainly semi-structured documents.	Useful when a large volume of very diverse data has to be collected and potentially analysed in realtime (eg customer analytics).	MongoDB, Couchbase, MarkLogic

WHAT IS THE DIFFERENCE BETWEEN A DATA WAREHOUSE AND A DATA LAKE ARCHITECTURE?

- **Data warehouse:** Data warehouses relate to relational database models in the same way as relational database models relate to structured data. Accordingly, as companies have mainly worked with structured data and relational database management systems in the past, the data warehouse has traditionally been the architecture of choice. This has brought about similar advantages and disadvantages as with relational databases, such as the need for a well-defined schema, the clear tabular structure and interconnectivity among database tables as well as the lack in flexibility and scalability. A data warehouse forces you by design to structure your data and think about the implications of the respective structure beforehand.

- **Data lake:** With the rise in the importance of unstructured data and NoSQL database systems, other forms of architecture layouts have become necessary. The data lake architecture allows for the storage of raw data in all types of forms, such as video or document files, sensor or drone data, satellite images and any other kind of data that you collect in your company. Here the lake analogy becomes evident: you can store anything in your data lake without having to transform it in some way as you would have to do in a data warehouse where you have to define a schema for each database that you incorporate into the data warehouse. While this is a great advantage that allows for storing large amounts of data without having to think about how to structure and organize it, it also involves the risk of littering the data lake with all kinds of data that ultimately turn the data lake into a data swamp. In this data swamp, nobody knows what data is in there and how it could be used, which would not generate any value for the company.

Extracting data from source systems

The data platform obtains data from a number of different databases using data pipelines. Batch loads are the default way of moving data from source systems to the data platform, unless data needs to be up-to-date constantly. In this case, a data streaming architecture is needed, in which any changes in the data source in terms of new or updated data is immediately communicated to the data platform to keep it up to date. For data streaming, there are tools and open source software that provide a great basis such as, for example, Kafka, Amazon Kinesis, Google Cloud Dataflow, Apache Storm, IBM Streaming Analytics, Microsoft Azure Stream Analytics and StreamSQL. These tools allow a near real-time loading of data into the data platform. Whenever there is no harm in data coming by batch a few hours later, a streaming architecture is not needed. Somewhere in between are micro-batch loads, which are batch loads that are scheduled constantly during the day to keep the data up to date. They still have some minor delays, eg they can refresh data in around five minutes, but they deliver much more up-to-date data than traditional batch loads. In any case, a high degree of automation of the data pipelines is crucial to realize a lean DevOps and MLOps approach and to reduce manual work significantly.

WHAT IS THE DIFFERENCE BETWEEN BATCH LOADS AND DATA STREAMING?

- **Batch loads:** Data loads are usually executed via batch load by simply copying the raw data as it is at the data source, which means that there is a regular time when all new and changed data is loaded into the data platform. See next section for tools.

- **Data streaming:** Data streaming is focused on processing data in real time. Streaming transmits, ingests and processes data continuously rather than in batches

---

Transforming and loading data

All processes require a number of transformations, such as cleaning and correcting data in terms of formats or types and omitting data that is not needed for the respective business problem or use case. Oftentimes, data engineers build data pipelines and data transformations manually by using programming languages such as Java and Python. Tools can support data engineers to move and transform data to and on the data platform easier, faster and more transparently and require less maintenance effort. There are many established tools, for example, from vendors like Talend, IBM and Informatica, which cover the entire process of getting data from the source systems into the data platform, usually by applying an ETL logic (see box below). They come with a very broad set of functionalities and are typically designed to be used in a low-code environment, for example by using drag and drop to design data pipelines, which means that administrators and users do not have to be software developers to take advantage of the tool. While most of these tools also support cloud deployments and cloud data platforms, their primary focus has in the past been to support on-premise data warehouses. More and more tech companies are using these next-generation cloud native ELT tools as their main way of getting data into the data platform and executing data transformations. They are usually based on open source frameworks and are primarily built for cloud data platforms. Each of these tools is more lightweight and tends to focus on one particular part of the data acquisition process. Applications like, for example, Fivetran and Stitch can be used to extract and load data from many different sources as micro batches, while tools like DataForm and DBT can support data transformations when data is already loaded into the data platform. Many tools allow us to observe changes in the data structure of the data source and provide notifications when any transformations done on the data platform need to be adapted.

WHAT IS THE DIFFERENCE BETWEEN ETL AND ELT?

- **Extract transform load (ETL):** Data needs to be transformed into the final format first, before it is loaded into the platform, so the processing steps would have the sequence extract, transform and load.

- **Extract load transform (ELT):** Untransformed data is loaded completely into the data platform first, and then further transformed into structured well-defined tables to enable easy consumption of data.

Choosing the data infrastructure environment

The final and more superordinate design decision refers to the choice of the data infrastructure. You can choose among the two major options of public cloud and on-premise solutions (with a number of hybrid forms in between these two). In terms of use cases related to data products, cloud solutions provide a number of advantages compared to on-premise solutions, since they are very flexible, can be easily scaled up and benefit from a large ecosystem of software services. They also ensure agility, innovation and performance. Especially when dealing with large and fluctuating amounts and types of data and machine learning algorithms, public cloud infrastructure can provide major advantages compared to on-premise infrastructure.

There are at least three public cloud providers that are worth mentioning with regard to data platforms and data product development: Amazon Web Services,[1] Google Cloud Platform[2] and Microsoft Azure.[3] All three public cloud providers are quite comparable in terms of the quality and scale of the infrastructure and data platform offerings. When it comes to building the data platform itself, Google Cloud Platform offers the Cloud Bigtable service and Microsoft Azure the Synapse Analytics service; both are highly scalable and to a certain degree self managing in terms of infrastructure. Amazon Web Services (AWS) is currently the most frequently used cloud provider and offers the data warehouse service AWS Redshift. Snowflake is a virtual self-managing data warehouse. As the development of new cloud services by all three public cloud providers happens quite rapidly, it is important to follow the latest news on their offerings as things might change fast.

When dealing with particularly sensitive data, some organizations prefer hybrid solutions that store the most sensitive data in an on-premise setting. When moving customer data to the cloud, server locations should be chosen in the territory where the data comes from (eg Dublin or Frankfurt locations for European Union customers). For data from customers outside of the United States, customers usually need to sign a third-country clause before data can be uploaded into the public cloud, as US-based public cloud providers have the right for their US employees to provide some third-level support cases in special cases, even if the cloud location chosen is based in the European Union. Encrypting each data store with your own private key that is not generated or visible to the public cloud provider adds an extra level of security as it prevents employees of the public cloud provider from getting access to your data.

WHAT IS THE DIFFERENCE BETWEEN ON-PREMISE AND PUBLIC CLOUD INFRASTRUCTURE?

- **On-premise data infrastructure:** On-premise solutions mean that companies have their own IT infrastructure, including servers, on which the companies' software runs. The software can only be accessed via an intranet, not via the internet. On-premise infrastructure can be also provided as a virtual private cloud, which means that there is a middleware software that virtualizes and abstracts from the hardware stacks and requires less work in managing the infrastructure. Virtual private clouds are therefore easier to use and maintain compared to traditional on-premise infrastructure; however, they are not as scalable as public cloud solutions and do not benefit from existing public cloud ecosystems. Setting up and maintaining your own IT infrastructure requires major investments and talent resources that might better be spent elsewhere.

- **Cloud data infrastructure:** Public cloud solutions provide different levels of services (infrastructure, platform and software) with the help of massive amounts of computing power and storage that can be rented from a cloud provider on demand. Cloud providers usually provide services for building flexible and easily scalable data warehouses, offer many database options for structured and unstructured data, provide support for migrating, moving and integrating data and managing a data catalogue, and offer tools for machine learning and cognitive services including speech and voice recognition. Typically, you can access these services via the internet. An access management system and strong encryption, monitoring and security measures prevent unauthorized access. The great advantage of cloud infrastructure is that workflows can be highly automated by replacing repeatable tasks by infrastructure as code scripts and pipelines.

Setting up the architecture and development standards

The technical complexity of data products is naturally quite high compared to other software products, in particular as the complexity of creating, operating and retraining machine learning models comes on top of the usual complexity in software engineering and as data products typically require more and up-to-date data. It is therefore paramount to reduce complexity in data product development and operations whenever possible, which can be done through standardization of programming environments, languages and packages, through the establishment of standardized data transformations and feature stores and through the standardization of tools for business intelligence and machine learning.

STEPS FOR SETTING UP THE ARCHITECTURE AND DEVELOPMENT STANDARDS

1 Introduce MLOps to bring machine learning into production.

2 Standardize DevOps and MLOps environments.

3 Move towards a microservice architecture.

4 Standardize programming languages and packages.

5 Consider the use of business intelligence and machine learning tools.

Introducing MLOps to bring machine learning into production

One of the main reasons why very few data products come into production is the difficulty of deployment. In practice, more often than not the data scientist writes the model in a Jupyter notebook, achieves good results and sends the file over to the data engineer. The data scientist expects the data engineer to simply connect the model to the data pipeline and the model will work with real customer data in real time. Unfortunately, this wishful thinking rarely, if ever, works.

There are three solutions to overcome this difficulty. All three should work together to achieve the best outcome. These are organizational (cross-functional squads), process-oriented (MLOps) and technology-oriented (with software products). The concept of cross-functional squads was described in Chapter 5 and refers to having teams that are composed of members with complementary skills that work closely together on data products.

MLOps is a subset of DevOps and the application of DevOps principles to machine learning (see Chapter 4). The main point of DevOps is to establish principles that allow a close link between software development and operations. The same principles should be adhered to with machine learning. The difference between machine learning and software development is that machine learning is much less standardized and much more dynamic. A lot of processes happen simultaneously and independently of each other, but at the end of the day they need to be connected in order for the machine learning model to work. For instance, for a typical prediction algorithm to run you are likely to have several pipelines running at the same time. This would include the data pipeline, the feature pipeline or hyperparameter search pipeline, the model retrain pipeline, the prediction pipeline and possibly a software development pipeline, for example to display the model results for the user in the application.

All of these pipelines have a lifecycle of their own and need to be updated continuously. The data may change and require refinement and model adaptation. The search for features (hyperparameter search) constantly goes on with fresh data and may lead to the generation of new features that in turn change the model. The model itself needs to be updated continuously in order to update the latest model refinements and to avoid model drift. In machine learning, models tend to lose their accuracy over time and need to be updated continuously to prevent this from happening. Versions of software packages could change and require an update.

Evidently, all these pipelines need to be geared to each other, eg with tools like Kubeflow. They function as orchestrators that contain a number of machine learning tools and services that can be finetuned to work smoothly together.

Standardization of DevOps environments

When setting up the different programming environments, data engineers should agree with the team on the purpose as well as the suitable work mode for each environment. A commonly used approach is to have the development, test, stage and production environments in place. In the development environment, the most raw version of the data product is deployed right after it has been successfully tested in the local environment of the respective developer. The test environment serves as a quality control environment that thoroughly tests the newly deployed code, including the successful run-through of data pipelines and machine learning models. This can also include manual user tests as well as security tests. The stage environment should mirror the production environment as closely as possible. One aspect that will be difficult to mirror, though, will be the interaction with real customer traffic and, in some cases, the data volume. The potential friction arising from this difference can be mitigated by a thorough deployment strategy and adherence to the DevOps methodology.

Anchoring DevOps at the centre of the data architecture set-up requires setting up a robust configuration management, which ensures that in each environment, from development to test and stage to production, the same resource configurations are in place. The configuration management has the following elements: configuration management database, source code repository, artefact repository and a data and ML packages repository. The configuration management database contains all the information on the infrastructure, applications and services, including their relationships. Both the source code repository and the artefact repository store, manage and provide version control for a number of highly diverse files that contain crucial information to maintain the integrity of the data product during its entire lifecycle. The source code repository stores everything that is readable by humans, such as configuration files, source codes and scripts for test, build and deployment. It is also commonly referred to as version control, which emphasizes its main benefit – to be able to revert to an earlier version of the code if something goes wrong. Source code repositories often include additional useful features for documentation and collaboration. Popular source code repositories are GitHub, GitLab and SourceForge. Artefact repositories store machine-readable files, such as binary files, libraries and data for testing. Artefacts are secondary products that emerge during the software development process and contain metadata, such as dependencies or resources. Popular examples include JFrog Artifactory, Maven Artifact Repository and Sonatype Nexus. Data and ML packages provide frameworks for data scientists and data engineers to easier transform data and build machine learning models and will be covered in one of the next sections in more detail (see 'Standardizing programming languages and packages').

STANDARDIZATION OF CI/CD PIPELINES

An essential cornerstone of DevOps is continuous integration and continuous delivery. Practising continuous integration and continuous delivery means merging the code changes from the development branch into the main branch of the development environment and ultimately into the production environment on a frequent basis. This can be achieved by setting up deployment pipelines, which enable developers to conduct automated tests before their code is committed into the respective environment. If the tests fail, the code will not be committed and has to be refined. In a deployment pipeline, the different software deployment steps are split into tasks. If the deployment fails, the developer can quickly determine the source of the failure by examining which tasks were unsuccessful. The deployment pipeline should contain a variety of tests, such as unit tests and integration tests. Tools for establishing deployment pipelines include GitLab CI, Jenkins, Travis CI and Bamboo.

Moving towards a microservice architecture

DevOps relies on the principle of modularity, that is the division of a large amount of work (ie code, functions, modules, packages, products) into manageable subparts. If one of these subparts or components fails, it will not harm the other components. The most important of these modular structures are microservices and containers. Microservices subdivide a data product into separate services that can be developed, tested and deployed independently. A microservice architecture therefore facilitates continuous integration and continuous delivery, as it splits up the workload into smaller parts that can be divided among different teams. For instance, one microservice can consist of collecting user session logs, while another one analyses this information in real time (eg how likely is it that the user will buy product B when they have clicked on product A?) and the third microservice recommends a product article to the user based on these analyses. While microservices allow the service to be subdivided into smaller and functionally separable elements, containers essentially allow the application to be subdivided into separate pieces of software. The most famous container provider is Docker. Now, Docker containers are built based on container images. A container image comprises everything that an application needs in order to run, including its code, libraries, configuration files and dependencies. Once a container image is created, it is unchangeable. That is why a container image repository is needed that stores all container images as they progress during the data product lifecycle. In order to manage containers, their resource configuration and their interactions, you will need a container orchestration tool. Examples include Kubernetes, Docker Swarm or Amazon ECS. Moreover, data transformations within the data platform can also be inspired by microarchitecture development standards by componentizing data transformations based on reusable SQL code snippets with tools such as, for example, DBT and Data Forms.

AUTOMATION OF MICROSERVICE ARCHITECTURE COMPONENTS VIA SERVERLESS AND MLOPS

Docker and Kubernetes solutions require work for orchestration of the infrastructure they run on by data and MLOps engineers. Public cloud providers started to provide powerful services that enable ML and data engineers to deploy software code and machine learning models without worrying about the underlying infrastructure as they automatically scale up and down depending on the current workload. Examples of general purpose serverless functions are, most notably, Lambda on Amazon Web Services, Functions on Microsoft Azure and Cloud Functions on Google Cloud Platform. Moreover, MLOps services in public clouds such as Amazon Web Services SageMaker, Microsoft Azure Machine Learning Studio and Google Cloud Datalab make it easier to deploy machine learning models and operate and maintain them during their lifecycle.

Standardizing programming languages and packages

Using one programming language across teams has major advantages. It is much easier for ream members to review, reuse, test and adapt programming code, and team members can better replace and support each other when needed. The authors would therefore strongly recommend that one programming language is used in the data organization as a standard and additional programming languages are used only in a few exceptional cases, when it is really necessary to fulfil a task or there is a very strong reason to use another programming language in a particular situation. There are a number of programming languages that are used in machine learning and for building data products. They include Python, R, C++, Java, JavaScript, C# and Scala. Over recent years, Python has become the clear winner as the leading programming language in machine learning and data science, and should usually be considered the first choice.[4] Python is a simple and consistent general-purpose programming language, has the widest and most up-to-date breadth of libraries and frameworks (see box below), can be used on any platform and is currently the most used programming language for machine learning and data science with the biggest user community. It is also recommended that standards are set for programming packages and frameworks for machine learning and data product development to simplify code reviews, testing and maintenance, eg for designing neural networks one particular standard package should be chosen across the data organization. Using package managers should be good practice as well, since they help download and manage libraries and their dependencies. Popular package managers are NPM (Node.js and JavaScript), Anaconda (Python) and Maven (Java).

POPULAR PROGRAMMING PACKAGES AND FRAMEWORKS FOR PYTHON

- Data analysis and visualization: NumPy, SciPy, Pandas, Seaborn.
- Machine learning: TensorFlow, Keras, Scikit-learn, PyTorch, Spark MLlib, Theano.

- Computer vision: OpenCV, Scikit-image, Pillow, Dlib.
- Natural language processing: NLTK, spaCy, TextBlob, CoreNLP.
- User interface development: React, Angular, Vue, Elm.
- APIs and microservices: Flask, Django, Falcon, Jam.py, FastAPI.

One way of standardizing machine learning is by creating a joint feature store across the data organization. Every time machine learning models are brought into production, all feature variables that are used by the model are published in the feature store, so that they can be reused by other data scientists, which can lead to significant savings for data scientists who need less time for data preparation. Finally, having a common set of tools and development standards across the different stages of the data platform facilitates the deployment of machine learning models and requires less manual effort to move the machine learning model into a different stage.

Considering the usage of business intelligence and machine learning tools

Technologies and tool standards for business intelligence and machine learning need to be defined considering different types of data users and data usage. For each category, usually one tool should be chosen to avoid unnecessary complexity in the architecture and for the user. Business intelligence tools used to focus on reports and dashboards that were predefined by the IT departments based on the requirements of a business department. Today, such tools are increasingly replaced by a new generation of business intelligence tools that empower business users to create business intelligence insights and visualizations as self-service. Another tool category is tools that enable business users to do agile data integrations and transformations and even build and run machine learning models using drag and drop user interfaces that do not require any programming skills. Creating machine learning models requires, however, a good understanding of what the machine learning models do, how they work and what their limitations are. If an employee creates a machine learning model that prepares or even makes important business decisions, it can be dangerous if the machine learning model methodology is not well understood. Another category is powerful machine learning tools for data scientists with programming skills, which make it easier to create and scale machine learning models and push them into productive environments. Some tool providers even go so far as to start automating the tasks of a data scientist, a category of tools and frameworks known as AutoML, which can support data scientists to speed up development.

TOOL CATEGORIES AND EXAMPLES FOR BUSINESS INTELLIGENCE AND MACHINE LEARNING

- Business intelligence (BI) reports and dashboards: IBM Cognos, SAS Web Report Studio, MicroStrategy, SAP BW, Oracle BI.
- Self-service BI and visualization: Tableau, Microsoft Power BI, Qlik Sense, Looker.
- Machine learning (drag and drop): KNIME, Rapidminer, Dataiku, IBM SPSS, SAS Viya.
- Machine learning (programming): AWS Sagemaker, Microsoft Azure Machine Learning Studio, Google Cloud Datalab, H2O, Apache Mahout, Colab.
- Automated machine learning (AutoML): H2O Driverless AI, DataRobot, Google Cloud AutoML.

Regardless of the tools used, one should keep in mind that the current standard to develop machine learning applications is Python and that most packages are therefore designed and supported for this language. For business intelligence, there is currently no clear standard; however, there is a clear trend towards self-service BI and visualization tools to enable business users to run their own data analysis.

Implementing data and AI governance

Data products bring about huge growth and market opportunities and profoundly change consumers' lives, as the mighty data economy players like Google, Alibaba and Tencent demonstrate. Pressure on taking responsibility for data products and demands for exerting more control over them are therefore getting more pronounced. The ever-increasing regulatory requirements and customer demands for insights on what happens with their data and how algorithms reach their results put companies on the spot. This can also create great opportunities, because companies can differentiate themselves by incorporating control and protection mechanisms into their value proposition to build consumer trust. This will mean establishing thorough data and AI governance, irrespective of whether data products are used within a company or as a consumer product or service.

Data and AI governance has to form the very basis of your efforts to place data products in the centre of the company for two main reasons: to comply with external pressure and to create trust in AI-based decision-making. Data and AI governance is all about managing data and machine learning models as resources or assets. Good data and AI governance is also essential in order to convince internal stakeholders from applying AI systems and to obtain trust from customers who give consent to provide your company with their data. The goal of data and AI governance is to make data and AI more usable, accessible, understandable, explainable, controllable and trustable for all employees and systems in the organization. Hence, the main task of data managers is to implement data and AI governance in the most effective, secure and compliant way under consideration of all relevant legal and regulatory rules. Things that need to be managed comprise the acquisition of the right data for the data platform, providing secure and compliant access and ways to document data on the data platform, establishing rules for data and AI governance, data quality management, and data protection, security and compliance. While data governance is a relatively mature field with a number of well-established products and solutions, AI governance is just emerging and cannot draw on standardized methods and principles in the same way as data governance.

In the following sections we will outline the steps needed to establish data governance first, before addressing the key criteria of AI governance and first measures to implement this very recent issue. The steps in implementing data governance are as follows and will be explained in detail below:

- acquiring data;
- providing data access;
- introducing a data catalogue;
- managing data quality;
- assuring data security and data protection.

Acquiring data

Data sources of high business relevance should regularly load data into the data platform. An important task is to identify which data sources are actually of high business relevance and to prioritize in which order they get connected to the data platform. Data gaps in the data platform with high impact should be identified and actions defined to mitigate them on a regular basis. In many cases, important data is not collected yet and needs to be created, eg by capturing a new field in the user frontend of an existing application. In some cases, the permission or consent needs to be collected to be able to further use data. Tools that support data acquisition have already been covered in the previous section.

Providing data access

As highlighted above, many organizations aim to democratize the usage of data across the organization by making it available and usable to all employees while staying compliant with relevant legislative and regulatory frameworks. Data access processes for the data platform should be therefore implemented to enable fast and compliant access for employees and applications. The most important step is to decide whether an employee gets data access to a dataset or not. By default, employees should get access to data on the platform unless there is an important reason not to provide the data (eg when the data contains personal data or highly confidential data). Some sensitive data fields can be removed, masked or anonymized to make a dataset available across the organization. Role management systems have to be established in order to determine who gets access to which datasets and data fields. Data should not leave specified environments. Each data access should be monitored and logged systematically to ensure that irregularities and frauds are detected; for example, if someone suddenly downloads an unusually large amount of data or datasets that are usually not used by a specified role, the organization should investigate how the data is being used.

TOOL SUPPORT EXAMPLES FOR DATA ACCESS AND PROVISIONING MANAGEMENT

- Access management tools offer user self-service identity and password management, authentication of APIs and single sign on functionality including social sign-on (eg Google, Facebook). Example tool providers are Okta, Microsoft Azure, Ping Identity, Oracle, Amazon Web Services and IBM.

- Data governance and data catalogue tool providers such as, for example, Collibra, Informatica, and Alation, provide support for enabling more efficient data access and provisioning. For instance, Collibra provides functionality for employees that emulates a data shopping experience when browsing through the data catalogue with the possibility of checking out data items in a shopping basket.

- Self-service business intelligence tools such as, for example, Looker, Tableau, Qlik Sense or Microsoft Power BI, and more traditional business intelligence platforms such as, for example, SAP BW, IBM Cognos and SAS, allow employees to visualize data and download it as spreadsheets or CSV files.

Introducing a data catalogue

When data scientists are tasked with creating a machine learning model, challenges that are frequently experienced include finding the right datasets, deciphering what is actually inside the dataset and how the data fields should be interpreted. In practice, this often means running around departments and asking business and data experts in this particular domain for data and business definitions. Datasets that are not described well are therefore very difficult to use by people who have not worked with the dataset before. A lot of time and resources are wasted unnecessarily. The good news is that there is a sustainable solution to the problem: a data catalogue allows data about data (which also is called metadata) to be captured. In a data catalogue, all datasets that are in the data platform are described with regard to what the tables and data fields contain, the formats data fields need to follow, how tables are interlinked with other tables and when the data was last changed or updated. Not all metadata needs to be created manually. When data is loaded into the data platform, a lot of metadata can be automatically captured by logging and profiling the data. This system-generated data can also make it easier to understand where data comes from and what fields and values it contains.

TOOL SUPPORT EXAMPLES FOR METADATA MANAGEMENT AND DATA GOVERNANCE

Data governance and data catalogue tool providers such as, for example, Collibra, Informatica, OvalEdge, Alation, IBM, ASG, Alex Solutions, Infogix and Smartlogic, provide strong support for metadata management and some support for data governance. Functionalities differ quite a lot between the tools, and can include, for example:

- managing metadata and automatically generating it based on the logging and other data created by ETL/ELT tools;
- understanding how data flows through the organization through data lineage;
- functionalities to add business descriptions and taxonomies as annotations to the data in a business glossary;
- ways to manage data roles, responsibilities and workflows.

Managing data quality

Data provided to the data platform from the source systems is not always of high quality. If lower-quality data is used for analytics or machine learning this can create problems. Data quality is usually defined as its fitness for the intended usage. There are many dimensions of data quality, such as, for example, completeness, accuracy, timeliness, credibility and accessibility. Most of these dimensions can be measured with data quality metrics (although usually not very precisely). Data completeness, for example, can be measured by profiling the datasets and counting the number of fields that are empty or have 'null' values. Data accuracy can usually be assessed by using business rules to discover anomalies and defects, eg records that should contain the age of the corresponding customer should have values between 18 and 100 years (considering that customers need to be above 18 and usually do not turn more than 100 years old). The scope of data quality management should focus on datasets and data fields that are of higher value to the organization. Tools can help profile datasets and establish metrics and rules to measure data quality and create monitoring dashboards and warning messages to data managers and data users. The data quality on the data platform can thereby be managed and monitored. Moreover, when data quality problems are identified, it is the task of data managers to identify ways to improve data quality, for example by correcting data at source or changing the way data is captured. Some data quality problems can be fixed after the data has been collected, while others require the data to be re-captured, to remove data quality issues. Some tool providers have started to address the management of machine learning model output data quality, and this will become an important new field in the data discipline.

TOOLS TO SUPPORT DATA QUALITY MANAGEMENT

There are many dedicated tools for data quality provided by vendors such as, for example, SAP, Informatica, IBM, Talend, Oracle, SAS, Experian, Information Builders, Ataccama, Sodadata and Syncsort. They comprise different functionalities for data quality, which can include, for example:

- profiling data and defining and measuring data quality metrics;
- linking and merging different datasets;
- validating address data;
- cleansing data;
- enriching data;
- monitoring data quality;
- standardizing data.

Some of the data governance and data catalogue tool providers such as, for example, Collibra, Informatica and IBM provide functionalities to display data quality monitoring information and for managing data quality assessment, reporting and improvement workflows for data managers and data users.

Assuring data security and data protection

One important aspect of data governance is to ensure that data is managed in a secure and compliant way on the data platform. Data security is a subset of IT security and handles issues such as how to ensure that sensitive and confidential information is prevented from being shared (accidentally or through hacker attacks) with the public or with people who should not have access to the data. Processes for data protection, security and compliance should therefore be defined and enforced on the data platform in a user-friendly way. Each dataset, potentially even every data field in the dataset, needs to be classified according to its sensitivity and confidentiality. Data sensitivity is mostly focused around the concept of personal information:

- Does the data field contain personal information, such as, for example, age, postal and email addresses, phone numbers, GPS signals, personal preferences, etc, which are covered under national and international data protection laws and regulations?
- Does the data field contain data that is particularly sensitive and that requires even stronger protection, for example about health, religion and personal finances?

Personal information refers not only to customers, but covers the rights of any natural person about whom data is stored in the platform, including employees and suppliers. If the data contains personal information, the purposes of usage that are allowed for this data field need to be documented as well as the purposes that the data is currently used for, including the system in which the data field is used and the name and departments of the employees that have access to this data. Under many legislative systems (most notably the GDPR, see also page 219), customers (and, in fact, any natural persons) have a 'right to be forgotten', which means that all individuals have the right to ask for data about themselves to be deleted. They also have the right to be told how their data is used, by which systems and for which purposes.

Data confidentiality reflects another critical aspect, which is the question of whether a data field contains organizational secrets that need to be protected to retain competitive advantage, eg a secret formula for how a beverage is mixed or plans that show how a complex machine is constructed. Data access can be more restricted and monitored when data is sensitive and/or confidential. Roles and access rights need to be regularly reviewed and re-certified to prevent people that were previously allowed data access from accessing the sensitive or confidential data (for example, when employees move roles or departments or leave the company, or suppliers and freelancers are offboarded). The data platform needs to adhere to stricter technical security standards when sensitive and confidential data is stored and processed on the platform. Penetration tests and system upgrades need to be ensured and identity and access management needs to be managed more rigorously. The critical component of data security and compliance management is to train employees about rules and behaviours that are expected from them to stay compliant and to make employees more sensitive about potential attacks and frauds, and things they need to consider when using sensitive or compliant data fields.

TOOLS THAT SUPPORT DATA SECURITY AND PROTECTION
MANAGEMENT

- There are many software tools that help with data security, data
  protection and compliance processes such as, for example, Logic-Gate,
  AuditBoard, ZenGRC, Ostendio, Netwrix Auditor, Truce, CyberGRX and
  Nintex Promapp.

- A number of lightweight and more heavyweight tools (eg OneTrust,
  ZenGRC, Siftery GDPR Checker, Algolia GDPR Search Tool) support the
  implementation of data protection measures that are demanded by
  legislative and regulatory frameworks. Some data governance tools (eg
  Collibra, Informatica) also provide relevant functionality that can
  support the implementation of GDPR and other data protection
  frameworks.

- Access management tools from vendors like, for example, Okta,
  Microsoft Azure, Ping Identity, Oracle, Amazon Web Services and IBM
  provide many ways of enforcing secure access policies (eg two-factor
  authentication, complexity of passwords and frequent changes of
  passwords).

- Data infrastructure can be secured, for example, via encryption of data
  storage and data pipelines (eg AWS S3 storage can be fully encrypted).

Establishing AI governance to create trust in AI-based decision-making

Making data-driven decisions is the core principle for implementing
a data and AI driven culture in the enterprise (which will be addressed
in Chapter 7). This means in practice that every business decision
from the creation of strategic frameworks to the adjustment of KPIs
to the hiring of employees should be based on data and, if feasible, on
AI. However, it is one thing to understand that data and AI are important, but it is quite another matter to base the majority of business
decisions on them. Place yourself in the shoes of your stakeholders
and ask yourself how do you trust that your respective agent (eg
government, hospital, bank or the company that you hold shares in)
does the right thing related to your safety, health or money? Ultimately,
you have to trust that your agent makes the right decisions on the

topics that matter, explains these decisions and acts on them. Your trust is probably built on the assumption that the following principles for the decision process are adhered to:

- **Quality:** The decision is of high quality.
- **Transparency:** The decision is explainable.
- **Control:** The decision process is monitored and controlled.

Both quality and transparency require control mechanisms. Control mechanisms ensure that the decision-making process is conducted in the right way from end to end, starting with the foundation that the decision basis is working correctly (data and expertise), decisions are prioritized according to relevance, provisions are made to impose impartiality and to balance interests and the whole decision process is monitored, including during the execution phase, to keep track and trigger a response in case something goes wrong. Every decision also needs to be in line with corporate values, irrespective of whether it is made by humans, by machines or in collaboration between the two. Accordingly, data and AI governance means that for the entire data product value chain, from the data acquisition to the data processing, feature selection and machine learning model creation to training and model deployment, control mechanisms are in place that ensure that the data, labels, features and models reflect reality and do not contain biases or cross ethical boundaries.

The key criteria of AI governance are as follows:

- security;
- privacy;
- fairness;
- explainability;
- model quality;
- accountability;
- compliance.

The more critical a decision and the higher its impact, the more mechanisms are needed that ensure the correctness of the decision.

This brings us back to the issue of why it is inherently difficult to move data products from the research lab into production – because here it is indeed becoming a reality, with actual customers caring about their data (security and privacy) and asking, for example, why they have been given a low credit score (fairness and explainability), business owners and stakeholders asking for the model performance (model quality) and who is responsible if something goes wrong (accountability), and regulators preparing the respective laws and rules for all of these aspects (security, privacy, fairness, explainability, quality and accountability).

It should also be noted that the definition of model quality itself can differ depending on the use case. High model quality could involve high accuracy, but it could also involve high fairness. In many cases, there is a trade-off between accuracy and fairness and it is up to the business owner to decide which of the two the ML model should prioritize. Finding the right metrics for determining model quality is a major undertaking in itself that requires aligning business, compliance and technical experts. Accuracy is an obvious all-round metric that tells you how many of your predictions are correct related to all of your predictions. However, it does not tell you much about the cases that went wrong. There are two types of mistakes your model could make: a type I error is to classify something as positive, even though it is negative (false positive), and a type II error is to classify something as negative, even though it is positive (false negative). For fraud detection use cases, you will probably aim to minimize the undetected fraud cases, ie the false negatives, because these errors will be more costly for your business than the other way around. For customer churn prediction use cases, your target metrics might be reversed in the sense that you are likely to aim for a low number of false positives. Targeting customers to prevent them from cancelling their subscription with your company even though they had no intention of doing so might be costlier than 'forgetting' to contact some customers who want to cancel their subscription. In summary, there are always trade-offs between metrics, and choosing the right metrics for model quality is all about determining which kinds of mistakes are more costly for your business that you should therefore try to reduce.

> ### REPUTATIONAL HARM CAUSED BY AI BIAS AT AMAZON'S RECRUITING SYSTEM
>
> An Amazon AI recruiting system was biased against female applicants. Words like 'women's' and 'women's chess club captain' reduced the chances of success for a candidate. This created reputational harm to Amazon in the press. The company reportedly stopped using these algorithms.[5]

The big tech companies have already started to react to the pressures by legislators and society with regard to the governance of data and AI. Apple put data privacy in the centre of their 2019 Worldwide Developer Conference by announcing a number of new services related to data privacy, such as Sign In with Apple.[6] In 2020 Google published their recommendations on responsible AI and IBM created an open source project on AI fairness.[7] An option to prevent bias in machine learning models and increase fairness in decision-making is to incorporate diversity in the data product team to counteract data and model biases, based on gender, age, educational background and other aspects of diversity. Other suggestions are to hire data ethics experts that keep an eye on the ethical aspects of the data products, and even to appoint a data and AI ethics committee[8] as well as to establish a human-in-the-loop decision-making process. However, these efforts are still in their early stages and further technological solutions are clearly needed.

CASE STUDY
Setting up the data platform and architecture at a manufacturing company

This case study deals with a steel manufacturing company which creates high-end perforated tubes, metal profiles and complex metal parts for a number of industries, including automotive and tool engineering. For many years, a small business intelligence team as part of IT has been charged with creating reports and dashboards in a traditional data warehouse and business intelligence on-premise tool environment. Due to several company acquisitions and mergers, the company now runs several data and business intelligence platforms on production sites that are not interconnected. Moreover, many important data sources have not been integrated into the data platforms yet, creating data silos that are difficult to overcome and that result in a plethora of data quality problems.

The leadership of the company struggles to get a clear view of current statuses, capacities, purchasing times, operational and product issues and delivery times at each of the production sites. At each production site, administrative processes are very manual and have a slow reaction time when unexpected things occur. There is a general need for a better prediction of demand and capacities and a faster detection of potential operational and product issues.

Therefore, a data team consisting of eight people – three data engineers, two data analysts, one data manager and two data scientists – is set up to deal with these challenges. After assessing the situation, the incoming data engineers start to build a data platform in the public cloud. A tool is introduced which connects to the different existing data platforms and source systems with a large number of adapters, and manages data extracts. The most relevant data sources that have not been loaded to any of the existing data platforms are identified and are also connected to the new cloud-based data platform. A flexible and scalable cloud-based data storage system is used to store and then to transform the data with SQL and Python scripts once it is loaded into the cloud data platform. One data team member takes on the role of the data manager and starts to document all data loaded in order of priority in a common data catalogue with the support of subject matter experts from business and IT. For most important and most frequently used datasets, data quality rules are established after loading data into the new data platform.

Data from different production plants and business divisions is integrated and common business KPIs and metrics are defined to steer the business and provided via a newly introduced self-service BI and visualization tool by the data analysts in the team. The data scientists are tasked to increase the visibility and predictability of capacity problems, delivery and quality problems and supply chain problems. Together with the data engineer and the data manager, they identify the relevant datasets that they can use to transform them into machine learning model features and use them for their machine learning models. Each of the models addresses one of the problems and is deployed using a serverless function where the Python code runs including the used machine learning packages. The results of the models are stored in the cloud data platform and are displayed in the self-service BI and visualization tool to all decision-makers in the company, who now have a better visibility of suppliers, production plant performance and product quality. Early warning messages allow production plants to quickly react to arising issues and changes in the business.

Lessons learned and pitfalls for technology and governance

Data architecture is not finished when all available datasets are put into a data lake

This chapter has shown that building a data platform with clearly defined standards for data architecture is a multi-facet endeavour and requires many aspects to be implemented. Some organizations, however, focus solely on building a massive data lake and putting all enterprise-wide data they can find into this data lake. When data is not well governed and documented inside the data lake and the quality of the data is not managed well, the data lake can quickly contain lots of potentially interesting datasets that most people would not use, understand or trust. Moreover, the strategy of the data platform should also comprise how data pipelines are built, how data users access data and create insights and how machine learning models are trained and deployed. Frequently needed data integration and transformation steps should be standardized and provided as refined and more structured data to data users and algorithms. Access and security processes and monitoring ensures compliance and safety for the data platform. Finally, standards for programming environments ensure that DevOps and MLOps principles are adhered to, which avoids unnecessary extra work, errors and bugs.

It is better to build the data platform on a public cloud infrastructure (if you can)

In many situations, it can be reasonable or necessary to build the data platform on an on-premise data infrastructure. For instance, a well-functioning on-premise data platform that fulfils most of your product requirements might already exist in your organization. Regulatory and legal rules might even prohibit storing data in a public cloud environment, or your company may not want to store data that contains company secrets in the public cloud. In most other cases, it usually makes sense to use a major public cloud provider as data infrastructure for the data platform. Public clouds comply with very high security and availability standards, offer a great deal of flexibility, a higher degree of automation possibilities, pay-as-you-go and the ability to scale your applications around the globe with massive storage and computing power in seconds. Most importantly, complex machine learning model training and execution can be done without worrying about breaking the on-premise infrastructure capacity limits and slowing down other productive applications.

Try to rely on mainstream technologies, programming languages and packages

The data and AI space is moving at a breathtaking pace. Every day, new technologies, programming languages and software packages are published that seem to solve something better, faster or cheaper. Never underestimate how much your data scientists, data engineers and software developers love to play around with these new things. They would usually rather go for something new than stick with a technology, programming language or software package that has been around for a while. Also, data scientists, data engineers and software developers have personal preferences that contribute to their choice of certain technology, programming language or software package. From the perspective of the entire data organization, such decisions are often not optimal. The recommendation is to stick with technologies, programming languages and packages in your data platform that are more mainstream, which means that they are highly adopted in the data community or even treated as de facto standards (such as, for example, Python as programming language for data science and machine learning). The advantage is that such technologies, programming languages and packages are usually more robust and better tested, documented in much more detail with better training materials, and there are many people to turn to in online forums to help you with any questions. Moreover, it is unlikely that mainstream technologies, programming languages and packages will be discontinued, as they are used by a huge data and developer community.

Document everything related to the architecture of your data product

When setting up the architecture of your data product, all the decisions might seem clear-cut and natural. However, once the data product development has been under way for some time, you might question why a particular decision has been made and why a particular technology has been chosen. That is why it is important to document everything, from the kick-off workshop results on the structure of the data platform with the business stakeholders to the data engineer's draft of the database schema to the brainstorming session with the machine learning engineer on the configuration of the deployment pipeline. This will also help you structure your thoughts and facilitate discussions, and ensure that every team member can always look everything up in order to stick to it. Possible places for documentation could be an internal wiki page, a source code repository or any other documentation tool.

Checklist for technology and governance

The following checklist can be used as a template for the three phases of technology and governance, to identify whether any important aspects might have been missed out.

CHECKLIST

Data platform:

- flexible and adaptable physical data infrastructure;
- data storage for structured data;
- data storage for unstructured data;
- standard ways to extract, load and transform data supported by tools and data platform.

Architecture and development standards:

- MLOps is implemented;
- standard environment across stages;
- container and serverless standards set;
- standardized programming language;
- microarchitecture standards set;
- standardized data pipelines;
- selected standard packages for each problem;
- tool standards for business intelligence and machine learning.

Data and AI governance

- data acquisition into data platform managed;
- common and simple way of data access;
- automated data quality rules monitoring;
- joint data catalogue and metadata repository;
- data governance workflow management;
- data security on data platform monitored;
- compliance ensured on data platform;
- AI governance established;
- trust in AI-based decision-making ensured.

Summary and conclusion

This chapter provided a deep dive into the technology and governance aspects of driving digital transformation through data and AI. First of all, the data infrastructure and central data repositories need to be implemented to obtain data from different source systems, transform it into common data formats, store it in a safe and compliant way and provide the data to data consumers. In the second phase, architecture and development standards are defined for data products running on the data platform, including the way machine learning, business intelligence and software development are implemented and run on the data platform. Finally, data and AI governance need to be established and enforced. Building capabilities has to be complemented by culture change and transformation, which will be covered in the final chapter.

Notes

1   Amazon Web Services, Data and analytics, 2020. https://aws.amazon.com/de/solutionspace/big-data/ (archived at https://perma.cc/LG3F-NYZZ)

2   Google Cloud, Google Cloud Databases, 2020. https://cloud.google.com/products/databases (archived at https://perma.cc/CYR3-QS4T)

3   Microsoft Azure, Innovate faster with Azure data service, 2020. https://azure.microsoft.com/en-us/overview/data-platform/ (archived at https://perma.cc/5RAA-Q3G6)

4   Beklemysheva, A, Why use Python for AI and machine learning? Steel Kiwi, 2020. https://steelkiwi.com/blog/python-for-ai-and-machine-learning/ (archived at https://perma.cc/VE3D-9CP8); Voskoglou, C, What is the best programming language for machine learning? 2017. https://towardsdatascience.com/what-is-the-best-programming-language-for-machine-learning-a745c156d6b7 (archived at https://perma.cc/BKD4-KVL9)

5   Dastin, J, Amazon scraps secret AI recruiting tool that showed bias against women, *Reuters Technology News*, 10 October 2018. www.reuters.com/article/us-amazon-com-jobs-automation-insight/amazon-scraps-secret-ai-recruiting-tool-that-showed-bias-against-women-idUSKCN1MK08G (archived at https://perma.cc/56GG-GEH3)

6   Apple, Apple WWDC 2019 keynote in 13 minutes [video], 2019. www.youtube.com/watch?v=izSg1YUvpAA (archived at https://perma.cc/D67X-5MQU)

7   Google, Responsible AI practices, 2020. https://ai.google/responsibilities/responsible-ai-practices (archived at https://perma.cc/6SMW-PYAM); IBM, AI fairness 360 open source toolkit, 2020. https://aif360.mybluemix.net (archived at https://perma.cc/9WF8-PM7J)

8   Sandler, R and Basl, J, Building data and AI ethics committees, 2019. www.accenture.com/_acnmedia/pdf-107/accenture-ai-and-data-ethics-committee-report-11.pdf (archived at https://perma.cc/RV7D-T94G)

07

Transformation and culture

LEARNING OBJECTIVES FOR THIS CHAPTER

- Learn how to establish a data and AI driven culture.
- Learn how to successfully manage transformational change.
- Learn how to manage the implementation of the strategy and vision.
- Learn why trying to become the next Google is usually a bad idea.
- Learn why visionary leadership means walking the talk.
- Learn why changing how investments are made is a key part of culture change.
- Learn why being agile and disciplined are shared goals and not contradictions.

Key principles for transformation and culture

To reap the fruits of data and AI, organizations will need to change, and with every change, there comes resistance, in particular, by those who think that they might lose out. This applies to many employees who fear that their jobs might be threatened. A Gallup study in 2018 found that 73 per cent of US adults believe artificial intelligence will 'eliminate more jobs than it creates',[1] and many experts agree. McKinsey predicted up to 73 million US job losses by 2030 through AI.[2] Some argue that most jobs will still exist in the future but they will change,[3] while research company Gartner claimed that more jobs will be created than destroyed by AI.[4] Organizations will need to embrace the changes associated with the current wave of digitization. In order to do so, they will need to adapt their structural frameworks, ranging from value statements, strategy and organizational structures to processes, as already discussed throughout the book. In its core, corporate values need to be adapted to the age of data and AI. Corporate values need to reflect two opposing trends: to be open, creative, virtual and experimental, and to align with new regulatory requirements and apply thorough control and governance mechanisms with data and AI. Organizations are shaped by people, so the changes in the business vision need to be accompanied by and need to translate to the adaptation of company culture, the direction from the top, employees and their habits. These processes are also vice versa, because employees bring in their experiences to adapt the organization's culture.

Going along with the organizational transformation is the establishment of a data and AI driven culture in the enterprise. This contains two elements: understanding the importance of data and AI, and making business decisions on the basis of data and AI. To achieve this cultural change, you will need to establish trust in data and AI and make them tangible and fun to work with. Trust can be achieved by establishing mechanisms related to data and AI governance, quality and transparency.

Transformational changes alter not only what we do, but also how we do it. Going about these adaptations and making digital transformation with data and AI a reality therefore involves major efforts related to transformational change management. Change management is usually required when a company experiences a challenge and has to react accordingly. For instance, a merger with another company requires a redesign of the organizational set-up, a reputation scandal might force them to change their culture and processes, while a recession demands radical cost-cutting measures. The stakes for digital transformation are even higher than with the previous examples, because the expectation is that digital transformation tackles all of these types of change management simultaneously: it should change the value proposition, the organizational set-up, processes, culture and make the company more cost-efficient and resilient. This makes it all the more important to adapt a very clear-cut business vision and transformation story that should state precisely why it is essential to safeguard the company's future early on. There are many soft and hard factors for managing transformational change that are necessary to bring the business vision and transformation story into life.

To achieve digital transformation with data and AI, we propose three stages for the transformation: to establish a data and AI organization first, and then gradually grow this centre and allow it to transform the rest of the organization and ultimately alter how humans and machines collaborate in the future. The transformation needs to be constantly monitored and adapted to ensure progress.

Digital transformation through data and AI is a long game and, at its heart, it is about how employees work alongside machines in an integrated way and utilizing data and digital technologies to reinvent their work processes.

FIGURE 7.1 The three phases of transformation and culture

Transformation and culture can be approached in three phases:

- **Growing a data and AI driven culture:** Every member of the organization should understand the importance of data and AI and base the majority of the business decisions on them. For this cultural change to succeed, trust in data and AI has to be established by implementing data and AI governance, and by enabling employees to actively use data and AI products, both by creating learning opportunities and by providing access to easy-to-use tools.

- **Successfully managing transformational change:** Empowerment of management and employees is crucial through leadership vision, training and education, data sharing and data products. Transformation and change also require changes in the way the organization operates, such as steering, investment and KPI adjustments, process and structural adaptations and new career progression criteria and incentive systems.

- **Implementing the strategy and vision:** Starting as a central data and AI organization, the strategy and vision should be diffused and spread throughout the organization and, finally, change the human and machine collaboration in the entire company.

Key principles for growing a data and AI driven culture

Data and AI will form the basis of the economy of the future and they will form the basis of every organization in the future. Data and AI should therefore be treated as core assets. They should be in the centre of a company's vision, structures and processes. This involves establishing a data and AI driven culture, which essentially means that every employee understands the importance of data and AI and bases their business decisions on them, and that corporate values are refined to incorporate new values, such as a culture of learning and experimentation and the company's positioning with regard to data and AI ethics. Companies receive mixed messages and feel pressure from two sides in terms of data and AI: on the one hand, they are expected to use data and AI as much as possible and scale data products as soon as possible; on the other hand, they are faced with more and more pressure to consider ethical aspects and apply ever tighter rules and regulations when using data and AI. Applying data and AI governance can help create trust, scale data and AI products and comply with rules and regulations at the same time. Finally, data and AI should be accessible by providing ample opportunities for employees to get started with them.

KEY PRINCIPLES
Growing a data and AI driven culture

- The importance of data has to be clearly communicated throughout the organization.

- Data and AI driven decisions should form the majority of the business decisions.

- Trust in these data and AI driven decisions has to be established by establishing data and AI governance, quality and control mechanisms.

- A culture of learning, experimentation and innovation is the basis of the digital transformation.

- Data and AI have to be tangible, fun and safe to work with for all employees, eg via easily accessible and usable self-service tools.

Key principles for successfully managing transformational change

Digital transformation is change management par excellence and requires a mind-shift for most employees and managers. The right communication, training and education across all levels of the organization are crucial for creating a strong data-driven culture. Employees and managers should be encouraged and empowered to participate in the data and AI transformation and come out as winners. The company's leadership plays a key role in clearly communicating the vision and transformation strategy and acting on it. Staff have to be actively engaged with an efficient communication plan and included in the planning process. Data products should be in the centre of the set-up throughout the whole lifecycle to make the change very tangible. Change management is also based around a number of harder factors that are a manifestation of the change in the company environment. Financing and steering decisions should clearly support the joint business vision and transformation strategy. Change is difficult for most humans, so it is desirable that everyone who supports the change should also benefit from it, which needs the right incentive system that motivates management and staff to participate.

KEY PRINCIPLES
Successfully managing transformational change

- CEO and top executives must drive the business vision and transformation story.
- Leadership communication is transparent and tailored to each group.
- Senior and middle management are involved in a clear role.
- Staff should be engaged in the process and their ideas should be taken seriously and acted upon, while work that has already been undertaken and the people involved should be honoured.
- Training and education is organized to gain support and develop digital talent.
- Recruiting and retaining digital talent at all levels is a top priority and needs special executive attention.
- The data and AI strategy needs to be translated into objectives and key results.
- Incentives for employees with rewards for a proactive and positive participation in the transformation process.

Key principles for implementing the strategy and vision

A successful data and AI transformation will evolve over time. It starts as a central organization and programme and diffuses more and more into each part of the organization as data products, capabilities and change management initiatives break up departmental silos and become closely integrated into the main company processes.

KEY PRINCIPLES
Implementing the strategy and vision

- Every transformation needs to start somewhere, with breaking up the first silos.
- The data and AI organization gradually diffuses into the rest of the organization through interdisciplinary collaboration.

- Running out of money and losing focus is a potential issue as the initial enthusiasm might dissolve after a few years. The progress of the transformation needs to be tracked and managed throughout the phases and requires continuous top executive attention.

- A new collaboration model between humans and machines needs to be developed over time.

Growing a data and AI driven culture

There is ample evidence that data and AI will form the basis of the economy of the future. Data and AI should therefore be treated as core assets and they should be entrenched in the centre of a company's vision, structures and processes. This involves establishing a data and AI driven culture, which essentially means that every employee understands the importance of data and AI and bases their business decisions on them. To make this happen, you will need to create a culture of experimentation and innovation in the company, adapt corporate values to reflect the emerging norms of the data economy and make data and AI tangible, safe and fun to work with.

Communicating the importance of data and AI and data-driven decision-making

Data should be the basis for all decisions made in the company, irrespective of whether they are made by humans, machines or in collaboration between humans and machines. Many corporate cultures do not put data at the centre of their decision-making, while decisions made on gut feeling prevail. The behaviour of top executives is of essential importance in this respect. If executives start demanding data and metrics to measure any decision-relevant aspect and if they visibly put weight on data, facts and reasoning when they make decisions, this will gradually trickle down through the organization. This applies equally to the usage of dashboards with metrics as the main basis for human-based decision-making. The usage of machine-based decision-making should be advocated and ensured whenever machines provide a sufficiently high and trustable decision quality in a particular domain or type of decision.

In addition, extensive training should be conducted in order to provide each employee with the necessary data familiarity. Data should not be something abstract that resides in the data warehouse and that is not important for the individual, it should be something tangible and regarded as a valuable asset. Education and training could therefore be complemented with elements of incentivization where applicable. Finally, embedding the data and AI organization into the company and creating opportunities to allow business employees to work alongside data and AI professionals will allow the data-driven culture to spread into the organization, because, ideally, they will report back to their respective departments what they have learned from the data scientists and incorporate the new data-driven attitude into their daily work.

Every employee should be able to understand that the availability of the right data with suitable quality is the very foundation of digital transformation. Although this might seem self-evident, it is actually one of the most difficult undertakings in an organization, especially when the organization's business model has traditionally not been based on data products. It is natural that domain experts tend to assume that their respective area of expertise can be adapted to a high number of business problems and, accordingly, they will tend to prefer the tools and solutions that they are familiar with, even if a new situation with a data product has arisen that might require a different solution.

On a side note, tech teams that build software that traditionally have not included data products to a high extent need to create a better awareness of the importance of data and AI and understand how they work, too. Take, for example, the situation where a problem in the performance of the machine learning model has arisen. If the underlying cause is not properly assessed, every team member will first think of solutions that fit their respective role. For example, the team's software engineer will hypothesize that there is a problem in the deployment pipeline and its underlying code and might undertake to solve this problem by inspecting the relevant Terraform file that contains information on the infrastructure configuration. The business owner will suspect that the machine learning model has not been well designed in the first place and the UX designer will investigate whether the input demanded by the user for the generation of the required data does not correspond with the user's behaviour. Using different perspectives, mind you, to solve a problem is not problematic in itself. It will only be problematic if the data-related perspective is neglected and only thought of at the end. In our example, none of the involved parties realized that the underlying problem could be the data itself that should be adapted. If an organization is not data-driven, this type of situation will be the norm and not the exception and will inevitably lead to lags in digital transformation with data and AI.

Making investments into a culture of learning, experimentation and innovation

Once you enter the data and AI world, you might be taken aback, because at first it does seem very chaotic and stands in sharp contrast to the clear-cut, well-defined mechanisms of company organization, processes and structures. Similarly, it contrasts with the well-established principles and structures in the world of software development – even though both worlds are based on mathematics, code and logic. This is because decades of experiences have shaped both organizations in traditional industries and software development. The new area of data and AI is just emerging out of its originally small niche and although it promises to become incredibly powerful – and it partly shows major strength already in the form of the mighty global data players such as Google, Amazon, Facebook and the like – it still is very experimental and does not have stringent processes that could be considered main standards yet.

This makes it so much harder for enterprises to establish standardization in this new core area. It also provides the chance to experiment a lot – and this might be a good thing! This gives your enterprise the chance to try, test, fail and try again, and to learn a lot on the way. This might uplift your enterprise to a new level, on the inside in terms of structures and skills, on the outside in terms of visibility and thought leadership. Now, this means that the solid project management approach should still form the basis of your digital transformation strategy with data and AI. However, this classic approach should be complemented with some elements of experimentation, in terms of both methods and content. After all, your organization is about to undertake a new launch and requires some igniting sparks to start on this new path.

Mixing up the set of methods your organization works with can generate new ideas that could substantially enhance your digital transformation. For that, you could draw from a number of toolkits that are commonly used in startups and by UX practitioners and that emphasize the collaborative, interactive and agile nature of work related to data products and AI. Some of these methods might even become part of the lifecycle of your data products, as outlined above. By applying these methods to your digital transformation process, you truly implement some elements of the famous dynamic startup mentality into the organization that is beneficial in a number of ways. First, it entrenches the very basis of data product development into your organization, which comprises the continuous work with iterations, ie hypothesizing, testing, adapting and starting the circle again. When your employees become familiar with this method in the early phase of the transition, it will become much easier to implement this way of thinking later, for instance, when agile methodologies are implemented in other areas. Second, it makes the organization more attractive for employees who are drawn to these interactive ways of work. After some time, this would create a virtuous circle by drawing more and more employees to your organization that apply more and more of the new methods, making your company ever more agile and centred around data products.

EXAMPLES OF METHODS FOR EXPERIMENTING, CREATING AND TESTING NEW IDEAS FOR DIGITAL TRANSFORMATION WITH DATA AND AI:

- A/B testing;
- business prototyping;
- virtual collaboration and workshops;
- elements from design sprints, such as 6 Thinking Hats, Crazy 8s;
- customer interviews and co-creation.

A crucial factor for creating a culture of learning, experimentation and innovation is the adaptation of the steering and investment logic that are applied by corporate finance. Experimenting means to pay for learning, and organizational learning requires investment. When a data product is not implemented after validation because the validation has shown that it does not provide the expected value to the customers or to the company, it is not a failure. It is learning that allows you to build an even better data product in the future and avoid making big investments in products that would not work.

In terms of thought leadership in the outside world, experimentation provides you with the great opportunity to pave the way towards standardization by finding and defining the right methods, processes and tools. You have the great opportunity to bring some structure into the data and AI world and spread the word. You may want to let the world participate in your efforts for digital transformation with data and AI by showing your work in progress and the lessons learned, via speaking at conferences and writing blog posts.

Adapting corporate values for digital transformation

Corporate values are the fundamental beliefs upon which a company is based and which guide employee decisions. With the rapidly changing economic landscape brought about by the power of data and AI, companies will need to adapt their values to drive forward digital transformation. For inspiration, companies should closely examine the current trends in the tech industry. These trends are twofold and stem from opposing directions.

On the one hand, data and AI driven companies helped build an interconnected world that is characterized by the virtually unlimited exchange of data and the increasing application of machine learning models. This has influenced consumer behaviour; customers freely share their data in exchange for a service, for example obtaining recommendations based on their user profile. Consumer behaviour and spectacular reports from campus sites of Google and the like have influenced societal norms and allowed new modes of work and technologies to emerge, such as open source, virtual collaboration, high levels of experimentation, making decisions based on data and AI and new ways of transferring and storing data, such as data lake and cloud technologies. The top tech companies have also started to blur the boundaries between industries. Apple aiming to produce cars is only one of the more famous examples. In summary, every company needs to rethink their corporate values in the context of the following innovation drivers of the new data and AI economy:

- high levels of experimentation;
- open innovation and open source;
- virtual and cross-functional collaboration;
- data and AI driven decision-making;
- cloud and mobile native;
- customer centricity;
- blurring boundaries between industries.

Mastering data and AI, and being top of the class in the new data economy, leads to unprecedented concentration of wealth and power for the big tech companies like Amazon, Microsoft and Google. Consequently, on the other hand, concerns arise over who has access to and control over data originating from individuals, companies and governments (compare also Table 7.1). This mounts to concerns related to privacy, business secrets and national security.[5] Governments have started to formulate guidelines and to put regulatory restrictions on this new data economy, most notably in the European Union.

As a result, governments, traditional companies and consumer concerns create drivers in an opposite direction from the drivers outlined above that also have to be reflected in the corporate values:

- new regulatory and ethical requirements with regard to digital, data and AI (in essence, AI systems need to be responsible, explainable and controllable);
- movements to protect data about individuals, companies and countries from external access and prevent misuse of personal data inside the organization;
- calls for standardization (both regulatory and in terms of processes).

TABLE 7.1   Examples of regulations, legislations and guidelines concerning data and AI governance

Applicable to	Name	Main focus	Further reading
EU	GDPR	Data protection and privacy	General Data Protection Regulation 2018 (https://gdpr-info.eu/)
EU	EU Commission White Paper	AI explainability	European Commission White Paper on Artificial Intelligence (tinyurl.com/qugrdak)
UK	Data Protection Act	Data protection and privacy	Data Protection Act 2018 (tinyurl.com/yybsr8sa)
US	Algorithmic Accountability Act (introduced to Congress in 2019)	AI explainability	Congress 1st Session Wyden (tinyurl.com/y5k6zgnp) Article on related US legislation: A new bill would force companies to check their algorithms for bias (tinyurl.com/y2x3wra7)

The two opposing trends are likely to drive the formation of new corporate values and point to the future of organizations. The company that wants to be ready for the future will have to embrace them both. This will mean establishing an open and data and AI driven culture of collaboration within the company and being ready to adopt a data-centric instead of an industry-centric view in the market. This is vital to reap the new benefits created by data and AI, but also to apply thorough data and AI governance as outlined in the previous chapter.

Making data and AI tangible, and fun and safe to work with, for every employee

Eventually, in order to incorporate this way of data and AI driven decision-making into a large organization, you will need to make the usage of data and AI an insightful and pleasant tool for every member of the organization. Many employees are curious to try out the new workflows and to derive new insights from working with data and AI tools. By granting them the freedom to start playing around with them, at least a number of them will naturally start picking up the training required to use and understand these tools.

The main prerequisites are to provide access to data, a process that is commonly referred to as data democratization, and to establish the necessary infrastructure, ie a data platform with a high degree of standardization, as outlined in Chapter 6.

While these preparatory steps are under way, you can start by implementing processes and tools that make data and AI:

- beautiful (for example, through dashboards and visualizations);
- tangible (everyone can work with data, eg via self-service business intelligence tools or off-the-shelf analytics tools);
- impactful (by addressing the key business and user problems);
- controllable (through data and AI governance).

Successfully managing transformational change

The strategy for digital transformation with data and AI should carefully construct the respective set-up and project management for the following cornerstones. Each of these key points will be addressed in detail in the next few sections.

Cornerstones for successfully managing transformational change:

- expanding the team with digital talent on all levels and retaining them;
- tailoring transparent leadership communication to each stakeholder group;
- involving the entire management through motivation and expectation setting;
- actively engaging and empowering employees in the transformation;
- providing education and training to increase data and AI literacy;
- offering employees the right incentives and rewarding positive participation.

Expanding the team with digital talent on all levels and retaining them

Many organizations do not have the right management team to drive the digital transformation with data and AI. This starts at board and executive level, where usually most members do not have a strong digital background, and therefore cannot provide the right executive leadership during the digital transformation on their own. Hence, positions should be either re-filled/replaced with digital talent or they should be newly created (such as the chief digital officer or chief data officer). The first management hires are usually the most important ones, as no digital talent wants to join a company if they are the only ones in the company. Be prepared to pay 50–100 per cent above market level premium of salary to get the first few digital talents into your company. Once a small outstanding team has been established and an empowered data and AI strategy is in place, more talent will follow with salary levels that are much closer to the market level. There might also be great digital talent that you discover inside your own organization. By creating internal job postings and encouraging employees to apply for these new positions, one can track who is motivated to move to a digital job role and enable them with further training options to upgrade their skills. In general, all digital talents are highly in demand and need to be treated with care. A great business vision, agile culture and top management support can help, besides regular career recognition and offering potential for personal development for those who perform well. Finally, measuring employee satisfaction regularly provides opportunities to fix pain points that digital and data talent have and prevent them from leaving. On a side note, for organizational changes, we would recommend refraining from too much experimentation. Once you have joined unit A with unit B to form a new business unit, you should stick with this change for a while unless there is a major reason for further changing it. The organizational structure and the question of who is in charge build the very foundation of an employee's daily work life. Every change of this foundation creates friction and uncertainties that reduce job satisfaction, so it should be introduced with caution.

Tailoring transparent leadership communication to each stakeholder group

The foremost principle of an efficient communication strategy is transparency. Employees are highly interested in status updates and progress reports, because, after all, these changes will substantially affect their daily working lives. That is why it is important to communicate the current status of the change management process regularly and present not the final state for a given topic, but something that might be work in progress. By doing so, you give them the chance to see the direction that you are taking at an early stage and involve them in the process, so that they have the opportunity to contribute if they feel that the direction might be wrong. Communicating defined milestones is crucial to make success visible and to strengthen motivation and team spirit. This allows you to collect and demonstrate evidence for impact and display a number of small successes rather than one major success that is more unlikely.

Once you have applied the gospel of transformation, you should start taking base measurements and then start to take further measurements during every step to provide regular evidence to your leadership that your company is on the right track based on the expectations you have raised as part of your storytelling. Having evidence to show that corresponds to the expectation level of your storytelling in the beginning is a proof point that your story is right (at least so far). It increases the level of trust of your upper management in the digital transformation activities during the next phases as you move towards the defined target state. Even if business benefits are not high during the phase you are in right now, people will feel more assured that the high business benefits that come later are in the process of being achieved.

A great communication strategy takes into consideration content, timing and attitude of the delivered messages. A good mix of communication methods is also advisable. A lecture-type format is fine for presenting updates on the progress of the digital transformation, while town hall type meetings might be more suitable when you want to invite lively discussions. Town hall meetings allow two-way communication that invites employees to ask questions, raise concerns and discuss controversial topics openly. You should also keep in mind that people differ in their preferred types of information uptake. Some might prefer listening to a presentation, while others might prefer taking in written information, for example on an internal website that is updated regularly.

*Involving the entire management through motivation
and expectation setting*

In order to drive change across all organizational units, the relevant top, senior and middle managers have to be closely involved and should know what they are expected to contribute to the overall business vision and transformation story. It is the most important role of the CEO during change processes to align the entire management team with regard to the new business vision and the transformation strategy. After all, they will have to conduct the implementation of the data and AI strategy in their respective departments. First, you need to identify the stakeholders and get in touch with them to understand their perspective and possible concerns. Second, you should prioritize them according to their interest and power, and develop ways to incorporate them into your overall strategy. Now, you can think of ways to deal with each group. One approach to involve top, senior and middle management in the digital transformation process is to include them in a change management team that has specific tasks and responsibilities. The change management team should be cross-functional, so that different perspectives can be included. Needless to say, this should reflect diversity of backgrounds, gender and other measures of diversity.

Stakeholders with high power and a supporting attitude towards the digital transformation change programme should obtain a leading role in the change management team. They can serve as leaders and replicators to drive change within the organization. Stakeholders with high power and neutral attitude towards digital transformation could be included in the change management team, but with a slightly less exposed role than the previous group of senior management. Close one-on-one communication might be helpful to identify what might stop them from having a more positive attitude towards change, and this can be worked on to get them completely on board. Most importantly, for senior management with high power and strong opposition towards digital transformation, consistent communication efforts need to be made to find out what is causing the opposition, and this information should then be acted on. The reason for opposing digital transformation is usually the concern that the current high amount of power will be substantially eradicated as a result of the change process. By closely involving the affected stakeholders and keeping the channel of communication open you might be able to mitigate these concerns and find a solution that suits both sides. For example, a new role could be found that is equal in power and visibility to the previous role and suits the manager's competencies. However, if nothing works and the transformation receives constant opposition and undermines the change efforts, the CEO might need to take tough decisions, such as transferring the manager to a different position where the harm that they can do is minimized or, in the worst scenario, to encourage the opposing manager to leave the company to avoid significant harm being done to the change process.

Actively engaging and empowering employees in the transformation

Active staff engagement means to closely involve employees in the change process towards creating a data and AI driven culture and driving digital transformation. How do you organize employee engagement? Some employees might have a natural interest in working with data and AI and digital technologies and are more interested in contributing than others and they might be willing to serve as change agents who develop ideas and see them through. It is important to seek out these data and AI driven employees who might also have an entrepreneurial mindset, find the right role for them and provide them with the according mandate to conduct change. More often than not, this could be an employee with a slightly more junior role who may have a fresh perspective and the right attitude to critically examine the status quo in order to change it. These employees can often become the most important agents of change in your company as they come from the inside of the company and are, hence, knowledgeable about the business and current culture. You might be surprised by the potential that an employee shows once they are asked, for example, by a company-wide appeal to contribute to the data culture transformation by joining the change management team. Another possibility for involving employees in the process is to install or adapt the innovation or idea reporting system and encourage the contribution of ideas related to data, AI and digital transformation at the organization. For the more general involvement of employees in the digital transformation process, you could set up a regular but focused feedback system to obtain timelier and more specific employee feedback than the yearly company-wide survey.

In general, empowerment and recognition are the two main keys to obtain consistent employee engagement. Providing change agents with an official mandate is one of the first steps in achieving employee engagement in a highly hierarchical organization. If employees who are highly motivated to implement the new business vision for digital transformation with data and AI experience pushback from senior and middle management during their change agent activities, they will become demotivated. It is therefore essential to empower them accordingly, whether via a formal approach, a mentoring system or a combination of the two. The next steps for actual employee empowerment should be to mitigate strict formal structures, including hierarchies, the types of information exchange (replacing monologue presentations with active discussions) and access to specific systems (granting more junior employees access to systems and meetings that only senior levels have access to, or establishing new systems and meetings that everyone can participate in).

A fun way to engage employees in digital transformation could be to set up an internal competition or challenge to provide ideas for how to promote the adoption of data and AI in the company, for example in form of a growth or tech hackathon. That way, some employees might start to think about how they could contribute to the process or how company processes could be changed in that direction, encouraging an overall entrepreneurial spirit.

Providing education and training to increase data and AI literacy

One of the most effective change management initiatives is to offer training for everyone in the company to promote basic data and AI literacy. This training should be compulsory for each employee, including the members of the executive team and board of directors. Some training could also be tailored to specific business departments or groups (eg executive groups, technical groups, non-technical groups), some basic training courses could be made compulsory for everyone and more advanced training courses could be made voluntary.

In addition, there should be special training offers for employees who are interested in learning more. This could be done on a voluntary basis. Champions with a high data and AI affinity could be identified who could receive more training hours to follow their special interests. They could serve as role models for others to encourage them to do the same. Formal certificates and trainee programmes could complement these offers. Once a certain certification level is reached, you could offer these champions a transition to a role in the data and AI organization.

When you aim to implement a new data and AI tool in the organization, you can also call for employees to serve as promoters of this particular tool. Self-service analytics tools might be a good starting point, since they spread the data and AI culture in the organization (see above). These employees would receive specific training for these tools and could offer workshops and be available for questions from other employees who start working with these tools. The type of training should also be considered. More active training – such as design thinking exercises, group problem-solving, and hands-on hackathons – is usually more effective than conventional classroom training.

Offering employees the right incentives and rewarding positive participation

Last, but not least, active staff engagement requires recognition. Of course, this can be achieved by creating a rewarding system and providing financial or promotion-related incentives. These hard factors should be complemented with more social ways of recognition, that is, by giving employees a platform to present their achievements. Employees with a strong drive for supporting organizational change could be appointed as leaders of individual change initiatives that have a dedicated topic, such as investigating new modes of collaboration by setting up virtual teams that are distributed across different office locations. Another change initiative could be related to how to incorporate agile methodologies into the current project management work mode. During presentations on the current progress of the digital transformation with data and AI, the leaders of the change initiatives could present their progress as well. It is important that recognition acknowledges not only the current change initiatives, but also the work that has already been undertaken, either as preparation for the current digital transformation with data and AI or in a previous organizational set-up that served as the basis for the new data and AI organization.

Implementing the strategy and vision

We propose three main phases and corresponding modes of change to implement the new strategy and vision. In the beginning, the data and AI organization is brought to life as a new entity with an initial change process to break up silos by setting up cross-functional teams. These teams first will need to deliver tangible successes by implementing data products across the business and bring a part of the new business vision into reality. In the second phase, the rest of the company is slowly transformed with the help of the expanding data and AI organization and a broad range of data products in a process of ongoing change. In the final phase, data and AI will gradually transform the relationship between humans and machines in the workplace and require a reinvention of the job roles and reskilling of the workforce in the entire organization. Throughout the transformation, the progress needs to be tracked and impediments managed and given a lot of top executive attention.

CEO and top executives must drive the business vision and transformation story

Without strong leadership by the CEO, digital transformation with data and AI will fail. Evidence shows that if the CEO does not lead the way to a data-driven culture, the rest of the company will not adopt it themselves.[6] The leadership responsible for digital transformation with data and AI should display drive and passion for the corresponding business vision and change process. The majority of the employees in a traditional hierarchical organization will be fine with a top-down approach if the process and communication are transparent (see below). Most employees do not expect that they will be able to contribute to this process from day one, but they will expect some guidance from the leadership.

Employees also need to look up to their leaders in order to believe in their vision for a successful digital transformation and data and AI strategy. They will notice if top executives adopt the changes themselves and really lead by example. If the CEO announces that every employee will have to undertake compulsory data and AI training, leaders must also undertake the training. If they claim that the future of the company will depend on establishing a data and AI driven culture, they will have to live by the very principles of that data and AI driven culture. The leadership team driving digital transformation should have a clear agenda that focuses on business vision and strategy, including goals and measurement as well as people management, including senior and middle management and employees. They should deliver on their promises and make their efforts and process transparent. This means that the leadership team will have to clearly lay out the business vision and transformation story. In order to do so, they will need to draft and follow a clear communication strategy.

Every transformation needs to start somewhere, with breaking up the first silos

We believe that the data and AI organization should first be established as a separate unit or data and AI organization following the principles described in Chapter 3, for several reasons. First, this is where the data product can initially be applied, which is especially useful in organizations where data products are relatively new and the core business model is based on something entirely different, eg the production of chemicals in a chemical manufacturing company or offering project-based consulting services in a consulting company. Second, the capabilities are then built and tailored according to the exact needs of the data products, which is much more efficient than building a broad set of capabilities without any direct use. If this was the case, then questions would quickly arise why these resources are being spent without a direct use case, and resistance to digital transformation with data and AI would readily develop. Third, since the data and AI organization needs to collaborate closely with the different business departments, information is exchanged in both directions. The data and AI practitioners learn to understand the perspectives of the different business departments, and the different business departments learn to understand the data and AI side. By obtaining insights from different business departments, the data and AI organization can draw parallels, create synergies and implement data products spanning across a number of departments rather than just for the one department where the original idea for the data product came from. In turn, the business departments will be introduced to the data and AI driven culture, technologies and agile methods by collaborating with the data and AI organization on specific data products. The data and AI organization should be a strong unit in itself, so that employees with the right skills related to data and AI can work closely together. A strong unit dedicated to data and AI would have the mandate for building data and AI products without any day-to-day operative distractions, including unrelated performance metrics, and without departmental rivalries and silo thinking. A typical example of rivalry among departments and silo thinking would be if the head of department B says: 'I do not support Department A in their request for a data product budget increase, because that will ultimately mean that my department B will receive a smaller budget.' Situations like this will hinder efforts to build data products for an organization, not only on the department level, but also throughout the whole organization.

Now, once the data and AI organization has been successfully up and running for a while, there will be the daily interactions between it and the other business departments of the company, and product squads will include more and more employees from other business departments. The number of interactions will probably be relatively small, as only a few business departments will be involved at the beginning, as depicted in Figure 7.2 on the left-hand side. Nonetheless, the few employees from the business department who work closely with the employees in the data and AI organization will become familiar with their data and AI driven culture, their concepts, such as

FIGURE 7.2 How a data and AI organization will transform the whole organization over time

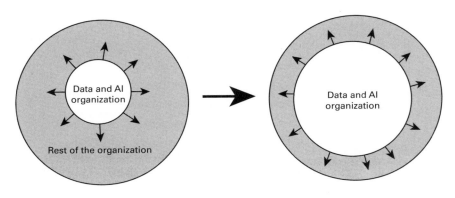

agile methodologies, and their technologies. Some of these employees will even aim to improve their data and AI skills and transfer to the data and AI organization. This will allow the data and AI organization to grow organically in the company.

A condition for this to happen is, of course, that the undertakings of the data and AI organization are seen to be a success. This can be achieved by selecting the appropriate data products in the beginning that can be quickly prototyped and show some results early, rather than starting with huge data products than span several departments, a number of datasets from different locations and require highly complicated machine learning models with a high chance of failure. The first data products should be easy and restricted to a small number of business departments each. They do not have to be on a global scale or revolutionize the complete sales process. It will be sufficient if these first data products solve a specific business problem, possibly reduce some costs or generate some revenue and, most importantly, make the life of a number of influential employees in one department easier. This will spread the word in the entire organization and other departments will become eager to work together with the new data and AI organization to tackle their business problems as well.

The data and AI organization diffuses into the rest of the organization through interdisciplinary collaboration

Over time, as different teams and departments work together with the data and AI organization and intertwine, it becomes more likely that data products will emerge that cover a number of different datasets from different departments. Now you can reap the rewards via network effects that characterize the data economy in general: the more data you have, the more business problems can be tackled with AI and the more insights can be derived! This will evidently lead to larger and more visible data products and demonstrate the usefulness of your data and AI organization in and outside the company to potential clients and talent. This will, in turn, attract more data and AI talent and your data of excellence will continue to grow. At some point, it might be useful to switch the organizational model to a hybrid model, which means that data scientists are still based in the data and AI organization, but they work for specific products within the business departments. Finally, as more and more data products are built throughout the entire organization and the culture becomes highly data and AI driven, you will want to switch to a decentralized model that may already have become a reality. Here, employees with data and AI skills work closely together with employees from the business side on a daily basis, but the differences become more and more blurry, as both sides have converged their culture and skillset to a very high extent.

The collaboration model between humans and machines will adapt over time

As the transformation continues, humans and machines will need to work more closely together. Industrialization has replaced with machine power many physical tasks previously performed by muscle power. Digitalization is increasingly replacing with artificial intelligence the cognitive tasks currently performed by human brains. Similar to industrialization, most work will not be fully replaced by machines, but rather supplemented. Think of washing machines, which still need humans to put the dirty laundry into and out of the machine, or the automotive assembly lines in which production workers and robots work alongside each other. This will change job requirements significantly for most employees, and will require many employees to be retrained to move from job roles that are declining in number to those that are increasing. According to McKinsey, 15 per cent of the global workforce, or about 400 million workers, will be affected in the period between 2016 and 2030, yet at the same time 21 to 33 per cent of the global workforce (around 555 million to 890 million jobs) will be created, with higher requirements in terms of technological, higher cognitive and social and emotional skills.[7] A common feature scenario involves machines that will support humans in doing their job by amplifying the cognitive or physical capabilities of human workers and by taking over interactions with customers and employees to save employees' time.[8]

Therefore, starting to reskill the proportion of employees who are willing and able to engage in such training is imperative for those companies that deeply care about the long-term well-being of their employees and is probably a very rewarding way to contribute to society. AI and software will be integrated into most workflows and processes that human employees perform, irrespective of whether it is in retail, the automotive industry, banking, consumer products or any other industry and irrespective of the actual job role. Designers will be supported by machine intelligence in product design, market researchers will collect deeper and faster customer insights with AI, assembly line workers will focus on fixing machines when they do not work, travel agents will consult customers that have problems on the website that cannot be fixed by a bot, and risk managers in banks will analyse risk data on a meta-level to inspect if there are any biases in the machine learning model.

Tracking and managing the transformation progress throughout the phases

When aiming for digital transformation and the implementation of a data and AI strategy, you might initially feel like you are reaching for the stars. The rewards are potentially magnificent, it is exciting and slightly daunting at the same time, which might leave you hesitating to define the first steps to get there. The transition work towards an organization that strongly adopts data and AI in their core business processes will most definitely require a change in working systems, whether they are related to organizational structure, processes or existing software products. Before you start to change a working system in your company, make sure that you do not diminish it completely before the new system is in place. Otherwise, this might create a vacuum that confuses employees and makes them question your leadership capabilities. For example, when the original IT department is supposed to be replaced by a new data product and AI department, you should not dissolve the old department and leave the remaining employees waiting for the new structure to emerge. Since organizational changes sometimes require a long time to implement, this might take months and will inevitably lead to frustration and a number of resignations. Tracking the progress and managing impediments that come up will be of the utmost importance. Top management needs to be deeply involved in every phase of the organization and must drive the change and allow any impediments to be removed. A solid project management approach allows you to make the results of your change management process tangible and to define the steps to reach them, also because small incremental changes are easier to achieve than a big bang. Setting specific milestones can be accompanied by defining your metrics and by communicating the respective results, keeping employees and stakeholders engaged and motivated. It is also useful to celebrate within larger organizational units when major milestones have been reached. This increases the visibility of success and sets a positive attitude towards the upcoming milestones.

CASE STUDY
Driving change with data products at a fashion company

A large fashion group embarked over a decade ago on its digital transformation journey. The renowned and high-performing consumer brands sell various fashion items in thousands of retail stores in more than 70 countries. Over 100,000 employees worked predominantly in these retail stores when the transformation started. The company realized at that time that there would be a massive shift towards online shopping as the traffic to stores was declining and reacted by providing a new vision for the business.

The new business vision for digital transformation had several focus points. The biggest one was to move from pure retail store sales to online sales. The move towards online, however, has struggled for a long time. A key problem in the digital transformation has been that most online sales came at the cost of losing sales in the retail store, meaning that the fashion group had to cannibalize their own core business. It required a lot of bold leadership, changes in organizational structure, business metrics, processes, investment strategies, career progressions and culture to accelerate and succeed in their digital journey.

Today, the fashion group operate online shopping in more than half of these countries via their digital marketplaces on a central online platform based on cloud, APIs and microservices producing nearly 15 per cent of its sales, and it is quickly expanding. Customer loyalty and AI are now key areas where the company invests, in particular, assortment planning to supply chain and sales. Thirty million members in its loyalty club allow them to track and keep in touch with a huge proportion of their customer base and sense changing customer demands faster.

Through thousands of online experiments that run continuously on the platform, marketing is increasingly optimized to improve engagement levels, conversion rates and customer lifetime value. The retail stores themselves have also been transformed, for example, by embedding digital technologies such as RFID to locate and manage the availability of items in the stores. Online sales today are heavily outperforming sales in retail stores in terms of growth. Leveraging the uniqueness of having both physical and online stores, the fashion group invested into providing a seamless omni-channel experience for customers, allowing an interplay between physical and online stores, for example through click-and-collect, scan-and-buy and online returns in store. In this way, the physical stores have become an asset even in a digital world.

Lessons learned and pitfalls for transformation and culture

Why trying to become the next Google is usually a bad idea

Alphabet, the parent company of Google, is one of the big tech companies, and with its $1 trillion market value one of the most valuable companies in the world. It has created impressive digital platforms for web search (Google), email (Gmail), online office applications (G Suite), videos (YouTube), storage (Google Drive), mobile devices (Android), cloud computing (Google Cloud Platform), navigation

(Google Maps), advertising (Google Adwords), website analytics (Google Analytics) and even self-driving car technology (Waymo) that are all dominant products in their segment. Many things can be learned from Google that can also bring your company forward: the way they provide the right creative environment for digital talents, how they ensure flat hierarchies by treating every employee as an equal when making decisions, how they empower facts over gut feel and finding consensus, how they nourish a strong engineering culture and engineering excellence, how product investments are managed, and their inspiring values. However, there are only a few winners in pure digital platforms and Google is clearly one of them. As inspirational as Google might be, it is extremely unlikely that your company will belong to the same club, so it is better to find a profitable niche in which your company can actually compete. It needs to be your very own business vision and transformation story, taking into account the uniqueness of your industry and your business. Setting up a data and AI organization is not enough. Data and AI should not become a solution looking for a problem. We recommend reading the great article from Catlin *et al* to understand the four general strategic options available for traditional enterprises for which becoming a pure play disruptor on a global scale like Google is not an option:[9]

1 smaller scale disruption on a separate playing field (eg by building a mobile commerce shop for only one of the fashion brands which targets younger audiences);

2 fast following (eg by moving to influencer marketing);

3 shifting resources to the new part of the business (eg by taking investment budget away from your printed newspaper business and putting it into online news portals);

4 large-scale disruption (eg by moving from normal cars to self-driving cars).

A strong business vision should fully embrace one of these options and should clearly guide the business's direction. The destination should be reachable while being ambitious, it should match your CEO's and board's ambition, and should adequately address the pressures and shifts in your industry.

Why visionary leadership means walking the talk

New corporate values such as customer centricity, cross-functional collaboration, data-driven decision-making and tolerance for experimentation and the new priorities set out in the transformation roadmap of the data and AI strategy need to be reflected in the day-to-day investment and management decisions and behaviours of executives. They are the role models for the rest of the company and everyone in the company will watch them carefully to see how seriously they really take the new business vision and transformation story. If executives and senior managers do not walk the talk, soon senior and middle management will follow by prioritizing the current issues of the legacy business, which is making the vast chunk of the profit, above the priorities of the transformation. Employees might perceive the entire transformation story as a great story for the press and shareholders, but not something that will actually be implemented and therefore become disengaged. Moreover, since most cash is still generated by the legacy organization, it is easy to fall into the trap of having more investments or job promotions in units that bring in the money rather than the ones who dedicate their working days to making the digital transformation happen. If career recognition is misaligned with the new business vision, the effect will be simple: everyone continues as if nothing had happened and digital talents who embrace the transformation process and would be willing to serve as agents of change will quickly leave the company.

Why changing how investments are made is a key part of culture change

A big danger for a successful transformation is that costs for the transformation are significantly underestimated or the ambition of the business vision exceeds by far the budget planned for the transformation programme. Most transformations need a lot of investment, much more than the usual investments. Running out of money is another potential issue as the initial enthusiasm might dissolve after a few years into the journey, especially as returns in new digital business models usually come only slowly. There is a need to act more like a venture capital investor when financing the programme. Some ideas will not work out, while others succeed, but you do not know which one will make it. So, the financing of data products should happen in stages; after each stage, there is a decision to be made whether to continue, to pivot or to terminate the products if they do not perform well. It is crucial to see every step as learning that should be documented. Stopping a data product does not equal dissolving a product squad team, who can be charged with designing the next data product that fits the team's long-term mission. For instance, if a team has the mission to increase customer loyalty in a particular fashion line, a data product that provides the next best offer algorithm based on the current data available might not prove to be effective. The team can then find either ways to build the algorithm in a completely different way by collecting new data on the website and by running online experiments or it can decide to come up with an entire new data product idea and validate whether this data product might be more successful in increasing customer loyalty. Excessive caution can be another major threat for the transformation, as it hinders the creation of a culture of learning, experimentation and innovation. It is often caused by an underlying fear of the unknown, which can be reduced by concrete initiatives that provide quick wins. Dividing the transformation marathon that can last a decade into a series of two to three year sprints helps keep the speed, investment and drive going.

Why being agile and disciplined are shared goals and not contradictions

What is more important – agility or discipline? This is a misleading question, as agility requires a lot of discipline and focus to succeed. Discipline is needed to stick to a business vision and the organizational set-up keeping it stable for a long time so agile teams can actually perform. Discipline is also necessary to focus on a well-managed portfolio of data products, capabilities and change activities that follow the priorities set in the data and AI strategy and transformation roadmap. This prevents spreading the resources and attention of agile teams out too thinly and losing track of what is important. Discipline is necessary to focus on the key metrics that measure the success of the missions of the respective agile teams. A key principle of agility is to inspect and adapt on a constant basis. You do not want to launch a new corporate strategy and then determine after a couple of months that this adaptation has not worked and everything should go back to as it was before. Rather than going back to the start, you could make some additional adjustments and incorporate the learning by making changes to the transformation roadmap.

Checklist for transformation and culture

Here comes a checklist for creating a data and AI driven culture and achieving transformative change.

CHECKLIST

Establishing a data and AI driven culture:

- Communicate the importance of data and AI and data-driven decision-making.
- Invest in a culture of learning, experimentation and innovation.
- Adapt corporate values for digital transformation.
- Make data and AI tangible, and fun and safe to work with, for every employee.

Successfully managing transformational change:

- Expand the team with digital talents on all levels and retain them.
- Tailor transparent leadership communication to each stakeholder group.
- Involve the entire management through motivation and expectation setting.
- Actively engage and empower employees in the transformation.
- Provide education and training to increase data and AI literacy.
- Give the right incentives for employees and reward positive participation.

Implementing the strategy and vision:

- Every transformation needs to start somewhere, with breaking up the first silos.
- The data and AI organization gradually diffuses into the rest of the organization through interdisciplinary collaboration.
- The new collaboration model between humans and machines needs to be developed over time.
- The progress of the transformation needs to be tracked and managed throughout the phases and requires continuous top executive attention.

Summary and conclusion

Our book has highlighted the various aspects that need to be tackled to successfully drive digital transformation through data and AI. The complexity of things that need to be considered is enormous. Leaders need to change what a company is doing (the business vision and corporate strategy, which includes the business model of the company and the new data product portfolio that needs to be delivered) and how a company is doing it (the capabilities, roles and responsibilities, organization, processes, technologies, governance and culture change) – all at the same time. At the end, only strong visionary leadership can make all of this happen by sharing a strong vision and leading by example, providing the right level of education and training, and providing an innovative ground for all employees to own their part of the transformation and to drive the transformation towards a data and AI driven company forward. Enterprises can make this happen if they are willing to embrace change and follow the inspiring paths that digital disruptors have paved for them. Building on the individual strengths and market advantages, enterprises can find their new position in the market and proactively reshape the future in their industry.

Notes

1 Vincent, J, Most Americans think artificial intelligence will destroy other people's jobs, not theirs, 7 March 2018. www.theverge.com/2018/3/7/17089904/ ai-job-loss-automation-survey-gallup (archived at https://perma.cc/P83S-SVM6)
2 Davidson, P, Automation could kill 73 million U.S. jobs by 2030, *USA Today*, 28 November 2017. https://eu.usatoday.com/story/money/2017/11/29/ automation-could-kill-73-million-u-s-jobs-2030/899878001/ (archived at https://perma.cc/Y6GA-V8C2)
3 Harrison, S, AI may not kill your job – just change it, *Wired*, 31 October 2019. www.wired.com/story/ai-not-kill-job-change-it/ (archived at https://perma.cc/ TMZ3-KUTJ)
4 Hiner, J, AI will eliminate 1.8m jobs but create 2.3m by 2020, claims Gartner, 2 October 2017. www.techrepublic.com/article/ai-will-eliminate-1-8m-jobs-but-create-2-3m-by-2020-claims-gartner/ (archived at https://perma.cc/MG2F-AVQQ)
5 Siegele, W, Special report: The data economy – A deluge of data is giving rise to a new economy, *The Economist*, 22 February 2020. www.economist.com/special-

report/2020/02/20/a-deluge-of-data-is-giving-rise-to-a-new-economy (archived at
https://perma.cc/K8VA-HCYM)

6 Davenport, T H and Mitta, N, How CEOs can lead a data-driven culture,
Harvard Business Review, March 2020

7 Manyika, J and Sneader, K, AI, automation, and the future of work: Ten things
to solve for, McKinsey Global Institute, June 2018

8 Wilson, H J and Daugherty, P R, Collaborative intelligence: humans and AI are
joining forces, *Harvard Business Review*, 2018, 96(4), pp 114–123

9 Catlin, T, Scanlan, J and Willmott, P, Raising your digital quotient, *McKinsey
Quarterly*, 2015, pp 1–14

INDEX